Decorative Wirework

50+ Ideas For Using Wire To Decorate Your Home, Yourself, or Your Favorite Things

Jane Davis

Published by

krause publications

700 East State Street • Iola, WI 54990-0001
715/445-2214 • FAX: 715/445-4087   www.krause.com

Please call or write for our free catalog of publications. Our toll-free number to place an order or obtain a free catalog is (800) 258-0929.

Library of Congress Catalog Number: 2001099524
ISBN: 0-87349-372-9

Photography and illustrations by Jane Davis.

Dedication

I dedicate this work to my sons: Jeff, Andrew, and Jonathan. They were the inspiration behind some of the most enjoyable projects on the pages that follow.

Acknowledgments

My three sons: Jeff, Andrew, and Jonathan.

◦ Thank you Carole Tripp for always being there to answer questions, give technical help, and be such a wonderful friend.

◦ Thank you Jack O'Brian at Artistic Wire Ltd. for providing much of the wire used for projects in this book.

◦ Thank you Maria Turner, my editor at Krause Publications, for your skillful and insightful editorial work on this book, and for your patience with me. It has been a pleasure working with you, and I hope we can work on another book soon.

◦ Thank you Donna Mummery at Krause for the beautiful page design.

◦ Thank you Amy Tincher-Durik, also at Krause, for helping to get this book under way.

◦ Thank you Rich, Jeff, Andrew, and Jonathan for being so wonderful and supportive. I love you.

◦ Thank you Kahlua, for not *always* sneaking back into the computer chair the moment I got up for a minute!

Kahlua

Table of Contents

Section 3: Projects for Your Home and Your Favorite Things

Introduction

The first encounter I remember with wire was coming across a pile of brightly banded telephone wire while my sister and I were walking home from school one day. My sister, Joan, made bracelets, earrings, and rings, which all the kids wanted to make, so we kept looking each day to find more colors to make into jewelry. It was so much fun, finding such a treasure, and then making it into something special.

But I don't remember anything about wire after that, except for jewelry classes when I was older. And those soon left my mind as well, until recently, when wirework books and projects in magazines caught my eye, just like those bright bands of color so long ago.

I've now jumped into wirework and fallen in love with all the possibilities that wire can become. Like all those different bands of color on telephone wire, there are many types of wirework to choose from today. Some wire artists take precious metal wire and carefully measure and twist it into fabulous jewelry fit for the finest jewelry stores. Others use tools, such as jigs and coiling devices, to make beads and chain links, forming a variety of fascinating jewelry. Others still, make wild, loose loops and turns, using them to accent arts and crafts of all kinds.

My wirework has taken the path of fewer tools and less measuring than the first two techniques, but more planning and specific wire paths than the last. I'm less concerned with precision than with the general design path of the wire as a whole. It's been an exciting and fun discovery process to find new ways to use this wonderful versatile material. And since the variety of wires to choose from has exploded in the marketplace, I've only begun to explore some of the possibilities.

Wirework itself is a fascinating craft medium. With a simple twist of a few lengths of wire, a beautiful work of art can be formed. However, it is a deceptive craft. At first it looks so easy to do, yet with wire and pliers in hand, you may find it difficult in the beginning.

A Note About Finished Sizes

All projects in this book list the finished size. This is a guideline only for you since you may wind your wire a little more tightly or loosely than I did, resulting in your projects being a different size than mine. Therefore, it's important to measure as you go so that you can make more or fewer links in your bracelet or necklace or a differing number of rounds in a woven lid ensuring that your project ends up fitting the intended wearer or object.

A collection of things to decorate with wire.

How to Use This Book

Many of the projects in this book are based on just a few basic techniques. The Basics section that follows lays out some of these techniques that are referred to throughout the book. If you are new to wirework, try out a few of the beginning projects with some inexpensive wire so you can become comfortable with the techniques. Once you've practiced, you will have no trouble with any of the other projects contained within this book.

This book strives to illustrate simple techniques of wirework, without forcing you to make it perfect the first time. You will need to practice with inexpensive wire first, until you get used to holding the pliers and wire so you can easily make the wire bend where you want it to, and then twist into your planned design. But soon, you may get hooked, just as I was, and want to try all the wire projects you can find.

With more than 50 projects for you to choose from, you'll get some fresh new ideas for wirework projects. So get out some pliers and wire and practice a few twists. Soon, you will be on your way to enjoying your own creations of jewelry and decorations for your home.

Section 1:
The Basics

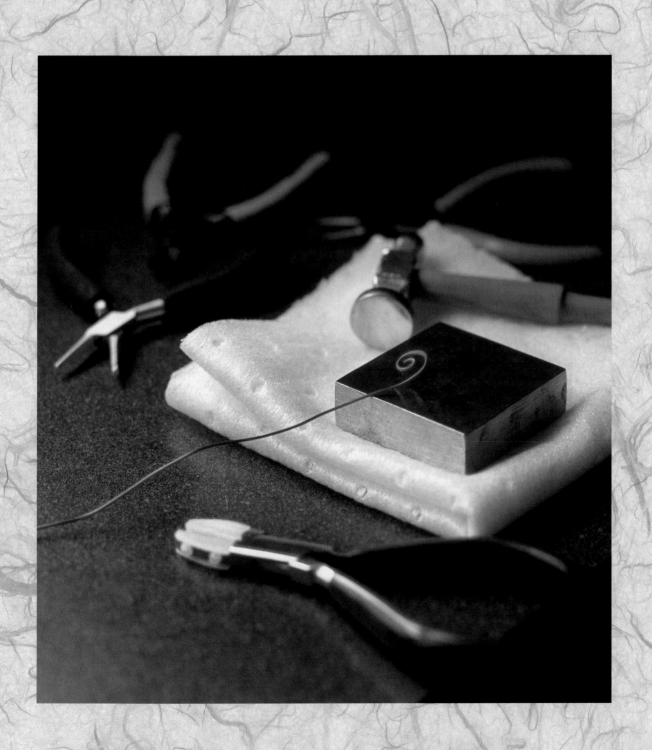

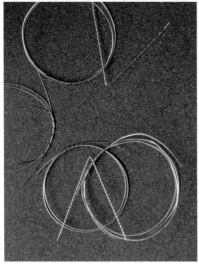

Clockwise from left: square, half-round, and round wire.

Wire and Its Properties
(sizes, types of metals and coatings, hard and soft properties)

Wire comes in a variety of different metals, thicknesses, colors, textures, and bendabilities. The most common type of craft wire is soft copper wire that has been coated with colored enamels. Most of the projects in this book are made from this type of wire, though some were made with sterling silver, brass, or bare copper.

After working with a variety of different wires, you may notice that some wire is stiffer than others, and that soft wire becomes hard in those places along its length after you've bent it a few times. This is because every time you bend, pull, or hammer wire, you affect the molecules of the wire, and it becomes harder at the point where you've worked with it.

Most craft wire is soft, while precious metal wire is sold in soft, half-hard, or hard states. I prefer working with soft wire, since it is easier on the hands.

Most craft wire is round when cut crosswise, but some wire is square. Precious metal wire can be round, half-round, square, triangular, beaded, or textured. Square and triangular wire is often twisted before using, giving the finished piece added texture next to round or untwisted wire.

Ready-Made Wire Components and Other Supplies

Ready-made clasps

You can construct just about any jewelry component made of wire. However, it's often easier, and saves time, to use ready-made jewelry findings. The following are some that are common in jewelry-making.

CLASPS: A device used to attach the ends of a necklace or bracelet together. A clasp can be a hook and loop, a ring and toggle, a screw-together lock, or even two magnets. Wirework hook and loop closures are easy and fun to make.

Ready-made ear wires

EAR WIRES: Loops used for pierced earrings.

HEAD PINS AND EYE PINS: Straight pieces of wire with a stop at one end. The stop can be a loop (eye pin), or a gem, a decoration, or a flat end that looks like the head of a nail (head pins). Head pins and eye pins are commonly used to string beads and make earrings. There are many other uses as well.

JUMP RINGS: Small circles of wire used to link design elements together or to make chains.

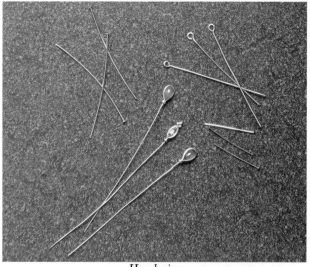

Head pins

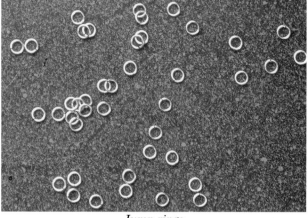

Jump rings

Pliers and Other Tools Used in Wirework

The tools you use for wirework are just as important as the wire you bend.

Pliers made of metal that isn't hard enough will bend as you work with them so that they will no longer come together all the way, rendering them useless for most processes.

Wire cutters that are not hard enough will soon get dents in the blade and will no longer make clean cuts through your wire, and may not even cut thick wire or very thin wire. Try to buy the best tools you can afford, asking the store clerks you buy from to suggest the best in quality.

All pliers for wirework should be flat along the inside of the jaws (the part where you hold the wire). The ridges on household pliers will mar the finish of any wire. I routinely tape my flat pliers, as an additional precaution, to help keep my wire from getting scratched.

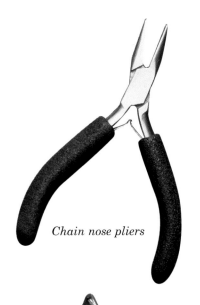

Chain nose pliers

CHAIN NOSE PLIERS: These pliers are flat on the inside of the jaw and rounded on the outside. They resemble household pliers, except they are smooth inside the jaws.

Chain nose bent pliers

CHAIN NOSE BENT PLIERS: This bent variation of chain nose pliers comes in handy for making bends in wire in tight places.

Chasing hammer

CHASING HAMMER: A chasing hammer has a ball shape at one end (the end where the nail remover usually is) and a slightly rounded head at the other end. The head is polished to a shiny finish. It's important to preserve this shiny finish. When you hammer wire to flatten it, you are making the impression of whatever you hit it with, so if your hammer has any scratches or dings, you will be putting those marks into your wire as well. When flattening with the hammer, always try to hit just the wire—not what the wire is on—or you may ding up your hammer.

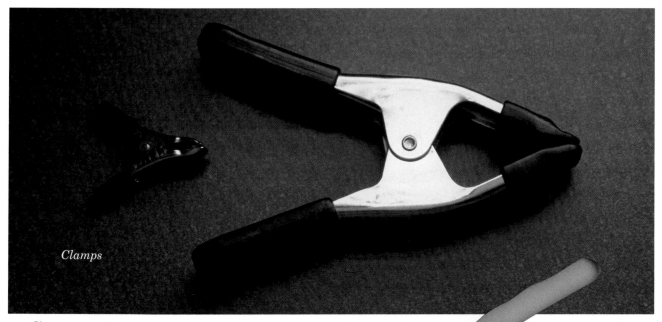

Clamps

CLAMPS: Clamps help hold wire in place while working and are especially useful when braiding wire.

Cutters

CUTTERS: Wire cutters can be wedged on both sides of the blade, or flat on one side and angled on the other side. Each type cuts the wire a little differently. If the blades are angled on both sides, both sides of the cut wire are angled to the middle. The better type, called "flush cut" wire cutters, cuts one side that's angled to the middle, but the other side is flat.

Flush-cut and angled cut ends of wire

FILES: Small jewelry files are often used to smooth the ends of cut wire and/or to round them.

Files

FLAT NOSE PLIERS: Flat nose pliers look rectangular at the end. They are flat both inside and out.

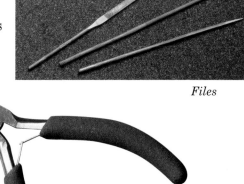

Flat nose pliers

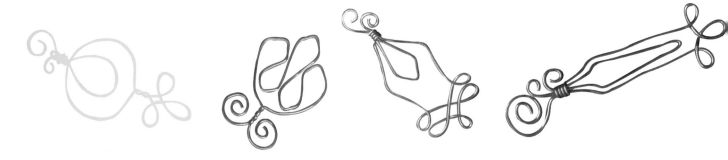

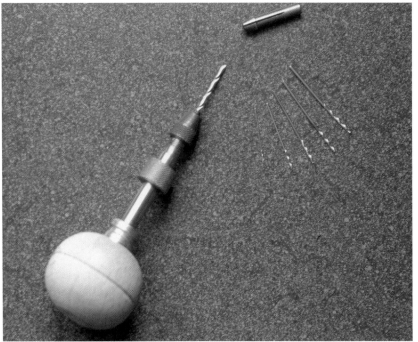

Handheld manual drill

HANDHELD MANUAL DRILL:

This is a great tool for making small holes in soft woods or plastics, so you can then insert your wire projects and glue them in place.

HANDHELD POWER ROTARY

TOOLS: A small handheld power drill is handy to have for a variety of tasks, including polishing wire, drilling small holes for wire to fit into, or grinding the end of wire instead of filing it smooth. There are a growing variety of these types of tools on the market, from battery-operated to high-end dental quality tools.

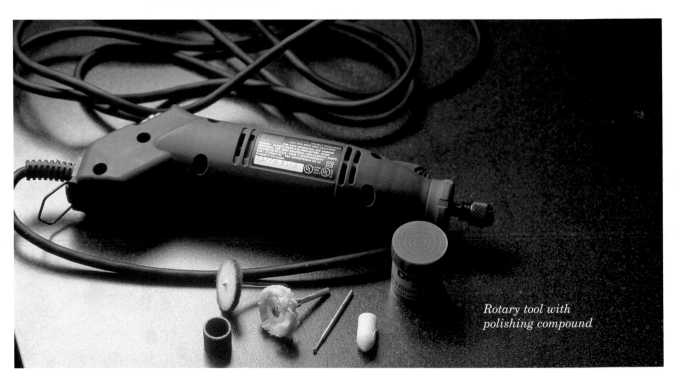

Rotary tool with polishing compound

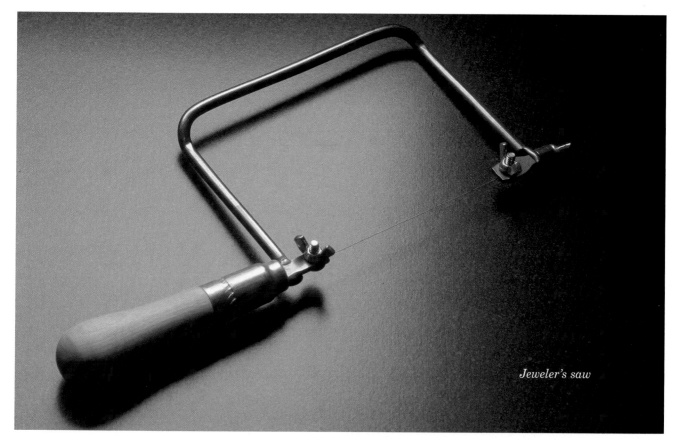

Jeweler's saw

JEWELER'S SAW: A jeweler's saw is a handheld saw with a very thin blade. Since it makes a nice clean cut through both sides of the wire, it is a good tool for making jump rings from a hand-wound spring.

NYLON JAW PLIERS: Nylon jaw pliers have replaceable nylon jaws that fit onto specially made pliers. They are a very handy tool used for straightening wire and hardening soft wire before beginning a project.

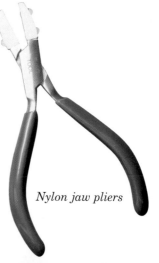

Nylon jaw pliers

To use the pliers, grab one end of your wire firmly with chain nose pliers and grip the wire with the nylon-jaw pliers right next to the first grip. Pull the wire with the nylon jaw pliers, sliding the nylon jaw pliers along the wire to the opposite end. Do this a few times, and it will straighten out any kinks in the wire and harden it as well.

PIN VISE: A pin vise is often used in wirework to twist two pieces of round wire together or to twist square wire. If you look at it closely you will see that it is basically a small drill, and the wire is like the bit.

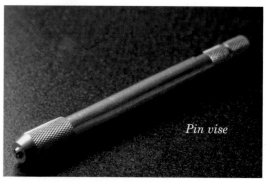

Pin vise

To twist wire, you screw the pin vise open, slide the wire in the hole, or collet, and screw the pin vise tightly until the wire is held in place. Then grab the other end of the wire with chain nose pliers and roll the pin vise along your thigh to twist the wire, keeping the wire taut while twisting.

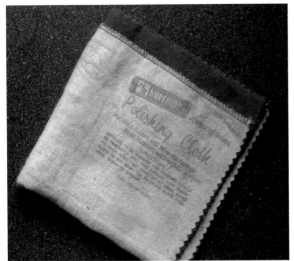
Polishing cloth

POLISHING CLOTH: There are several types of polishing cloths with different compounds in them for cleaning jewelry. A rouge cloth has a fine polishing compound used in the final stages of jewelry work for the final polish on the piece. Projects made with sterling silver, brass, or copper, will oxidize over time and need routine polishing.

Nylon bench block

POUNDING BLOCK OR BENCH BLOCK: A bench block is a small metal square or rectangle used as a base to hammer your wire. It is usually polished to a matte finish. Your wirework will have a shiny side (the hammer side) and a matte side (the pounding block side). You can also polish your pounding block so that both sides of the wire will be shiny when hammered.

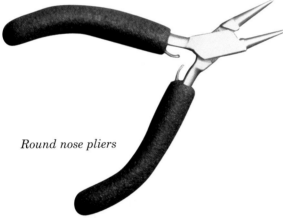
Round nose pliers

ROUND NOSE PLIERS: These pliers are round on both jaws, tapering to a smaller diameter at the point. They are used for curling wire into loops and spirals and for making smooth bends in wire. Varying sizes of loops are determined by where you grab the wire—at the small tip or at the larger base.

TAPE: Masking tape is an all-purpose tool, used to hold pieces in place while assembling and to cover the inside jaws of the pliers to protect the wire.

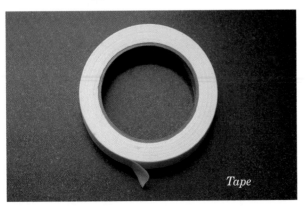
Tape

Other Tools

The tools previously mentioned are those I used to make the projects in this book. However, there are many more tools to help in wirework. The following is a short list of items that you may wish to try to help you with your wirework.

Crimping pliers

CRIMPING PLIERS: Needle nose pliers with a small indentation to crimp bands around wire.

JIGS: Boards with holes for pegs to insert and wind wire around.

Jump ring pliers

Jigs

JUMP RING PLIERS: Needle nose pliers with one hooked end to make it easy to open and close jump rings.

Preparation

When first learning to work with wire, there are two things that can make the process much easier and can help you to make more uniform components with, ideally, no scratch marks.

One is taping the chain nose pliers so it won't mar the wire. To do this, cut a small piece of masking tape, just a little larger than the surface of the inside of the pliers and carefully press it down and around the sides and tip, so there is a minimum amount of overlap.

The other precautionary measure is wrapping tape around the end of the round nose pliers, marking where the pliers are 1/8" in diameter (or whatever diameter that is required for the intended project). You can also mark them with a permanent marker. This will help when making a chain or other project where you need to make the same shape over and over again—especially when all must be the same size.

Cutting Wire

Safety when cutting wire is important because you will often cut small pieces of wire that can shoot out into the room. To prevent an accident, always hold both ends to be cut, or shield the cutter with your finger or hand so small bits of wire simply fall to the table, or, better yet, directly into a trash can.

Flattening Wire

Flattening wire projects, or parts of wire projects, can add texture to your piece by creating large or small flat surfaces that reflect light. Flattening also hardens the wire.

One way to flatten wire is by placing the wirework on a bench block and whacking down on the whole piece with another bench block. This method flattens and hardens the whole piece of wirework evenly.

Another way to flatten is to use a chasing hammer and bench block. With this method, you can pound all or part of the piece to different degrees of flatness. I used a chasing hammer and bench block to flatten parts, or sometimes all of the wirework, for projects in this book.

Care needs to be taken when pounding your work, though. If you flatten the wire too much, you can make it brittle, which may lead to breakage, or on color-coated craft wire, you may cause the color coating to flake or chip off. It is best to experiment with a piece of scrap wire before working with a finished project to see how much you can flatten it before it seems too brittle or the color flakes off.

Making Jump Rings

Jump rings are round rings of wire used to link elements of a design together, such as the ones connecting the beaded eye pins to the Bead-Fringed Lampshade on page 62. You can purchase jump rings or may want to make them yourself.

To make your own jump rings, wind wire (usually about 20- or 22-gauge) closely around a stick or thick wire, the diameter you want your jump rings to be. Slide the coil off the stick, and saw or cut the wire, as shown (Figure 1), using a jeweler's saw.

You can also cut the loops with a wire cutter, but you will need to re-cut the end that isn't flush cut, so the ends meet tightly together.

To open or close jump rings, always use two pliers and pivot one end of the jump ring away from you and the other end toward you, as shown (Figure 2). This way, you won't distort the circle shape of the jump ring, and the ends fit snugly together.

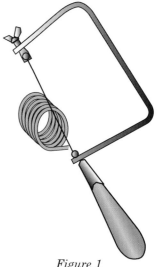

Figure 1

Figure 2

Samples of spirals: open and closed.

Making Spirals

The spiral form is a basic element of many wire projects. Spirals can be tightly curled, making a solid disk, or loosely coiled, with no wire touching itself—or a combination of the two.

To make a tight spiral, using round nose pliers and working from the spool, grab the end of the wire and make the smallest loop you can. Using chain nose pliers, press the loop tightly on itself (Figure 3).

Then grab the pressed loop with the chain nose pliers and begin pushing the wire around the loop with your thumb, pivoting the growing spiral in the pliers (Figure 4). Continue to the desired size, and then cut.

To make an open spiral, working from the spool, grab the end of the wire at ⅛" diameter on the round nose pliers. Make a loop about ⅛" diameter. When you have almost made a complete circle, grab the wire with the chain nose pliers and begin pushing the wire close to, but not touching, the circle (Figure 5). Continue pushing the wire close to the growing spiral as you pivot it in the pliers to the desired size. Then cut.

Figure 3

Figure 4

Figure 5

Making a Wrap

A wrap occurs when you wind wire tightly around one or more straight wires to hold them in place or to use as a decorative element. It takes practice to learn the correct amount of tension needed to wrap the wire without bending the straight wire, yet still getting a nice tight wrap. It's common at first to hold the straight wire too tightly so that it is marred in the process. A good way to practice this design technique is to make a linked bracelet or necklace of wire-wrapped loops.

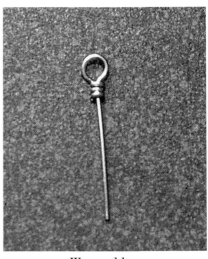

Wrapped loop

To make a wire-wrapped loop:

1 Working from the spool of 20-gauge wire, grab the wire with round nose pliers where it is about ⅛" in diameter, about 1½" from the end of the wire. Fold both ends of the wire around the pliers so they cross over each other (Figure 6).

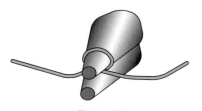

Figure 6

2 Grab the spool end of the wire with the tip of the round nose pliers, just inside the loop, and grab the spool wire with the chain nose pliers and bend it perpendicular to the loop (Figure 7).

Figure 7

3 Hold the loop with the chain nose pliers and grab the end of the tail with the round nose pliers. Wind the tail around the spool end of the wire three times close to the loop (Figure 8). Cut the tail close to the wrap.

Figure 8

Making a Clasp

A simple clasp is easier to make than you might think. Here are two ways to make the same clasp in 20-gauge wire, with a ¹⁄₁₂" hook.

Method 1:

1 Working from the spool, using the tip of the round nose pliers, bend the wire in half, 1" from the end. Use the chain nose pliers to press the fold tightly together (Figure 9).

Figure 9

2 About ¹⁄₁₆" from the end of the wire, use the chain nose pliers to bend the spool end of the wire at a 45-degree angle. Hold the wire just beyond the bend with the round nose pliers at ⅛" diameter of the pliers, and wind the wire around the pliers, making a circle (Figure 10). Cut the wire about 1½" from the circle.

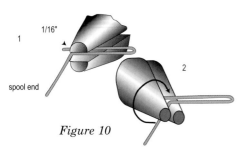

Figure 10

1/16"

1

spool end

2

3 Grab the circle with the chain nose pliers and the long tail with the round nose pliers, and wind the tail three times tightly around the two straight wires, creating "a wrap" (Figure 11). Cut the end close to your wrap and trim the straight wire protruding into the circle.

4 Using the round nose pliers, grab the straight loop in the middle and bend both ends up to meet each other. Grab the folded end about ⅛" from the fold and bend it up from the wrap, creating a hook (Figure 12).

Method 2:

1 Using the chain nose pliers, bend the wire to a 45-degree angle ⅛" from the end. Using the round nose pliers, grab the wire just beyond the bend at about ⅛" diameter on the pliers and wind the wire around the pliers and beyond the tail (Figure 13).

2 Hold the loop with the tip of the round nose pliers just before it crosses the tail. Grab the long tail with the chain nose pliers and pull the wire down so it is parallel to the tail (Figure 14).

3 Grab the long tail with the tip of the round nose pliers, about 1" from the loop, and fold the wire in half. Press the fold tight with the chain nose pliers (Figure 15).

4 With the chain nose pliers, hold the short and long tails and the folded wire about ⅛" from the loop. Grab the end of the long tail with the round nose pliers and wind it tightly around the shank of the loop, creating "a wrap" (Figure 16). Cut the long and short tails close to the wrap. Finish as in step 4 of Method 1.

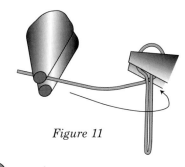

Figure 11

Figure 12

1/8"

Figure 13

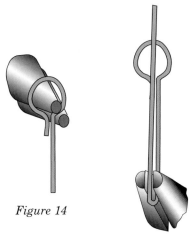

Figure 14

Figure 15

Figure 16

Section 2:

Jewelry Projects

Open Spiral Bracelet, Necklace, and Earrings

The simplicity of this design is what makes it so wonderful. And as you will see from this bracelet, matching necklace, and earrings, the possibilities for variations are endless. This is a great project for beginning wirework because the repetition of the elements gives you practice, yet you will be able to make beautiful jewelry the first time through.

FINISHED SIZES:
Bracelet, approximately 8½" long;
necklace, variable;
and earrings, approximately ½" long.

YOU WILL NEED

- 20-gauge soft wire on a spool (one spool will be enough to make all three projects)
- One pair of gold-toned ear wires
- Round nose pliers
- Chain nose pliers
- Wire cutters

Figure 1

Figure 3

Figure 4

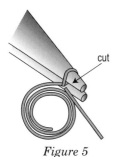

Figure 5

Figure 6

To make the bracelet:

1 Working from the spool, grab the end of the wire with the round nose pliers at ⅛" diameter and twist the wire around the piers to form a loop (Figure 1).

2 Grab the loop, as shown, with the chain nose pliers and gently push the wire around the loop with your thumb so that the wire spirals closely around the loop (Figure 2).

3 Reposition the chain nose pliers, and repeat the process until the wire is wrapped two-and-a-half times around (Figure 3).

4 Using the round nose pliers, grab the wire and bend it to a 90-degree angle from the spiral (Figure 4).

5 Now, holding the wire with the round nose pliers, wrap the wire around the round nose pliers, and then cut the wire flush with the spiral (Figure 5).

6 Repeat steps 1 through 4, sliding the previously made spiral onto the wire before step 4 (Figure 6) until the bracelet is the desired length, less ½".

7 Make a hook-style clasp, as shown on pages 20-21 of the Basic Techniques section, sliding the last link of the bracelet into the loop of the hook before making the wrap of the hook.

To make the necklace:

1 Follow the same process as for the bracelet, making the chain ½" less than the desired length.

2 Add the clasp. Or, if you make the necklace at least 24" long, you can omit the clasp and join the last link to the first for a continuous chain that can be worn as a necklace, or wrapped around your wrist for a multi-chained bracelet.

To make the earrings:

1 Follow the bracelet instructions to make one link.

2 Attach link to an earring by opening the earring loop as shown in Figure 7.

3 Repeat for a second earring.

Figure 7

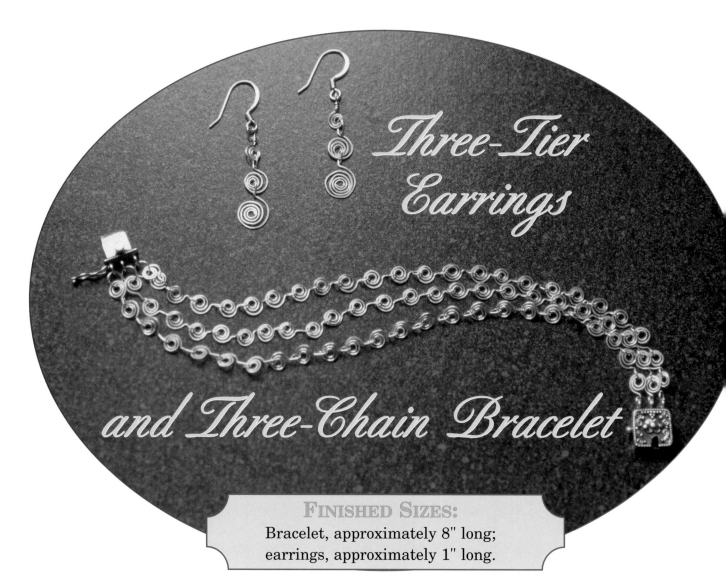

Three-Tier Earrings and Three-Chain Bracelet

FINISHED SIZES:
Bracelet, approximately 8" long;
earrings, approximately 1" long.

Changing to thin gauge sterling silver and adding a beautiful clasp transforms a simple chain into an elegant piece of jewelry. If you feel energetic, you could make a necklace, just like the bracelet, except make each chain five links longer than the one before so you have a delicate three-tiered necklace to go with your bracelet and earrings.

YOU WILL NEED

- Approximately 8 feet of 24-gauge sterling silver half-hard wire (this is enough for the bracelet and earrings)
- Sterling silver clasp with three loops on each end
- Pair of silver or silver-toned ear wires

- Round nose pliers
- Chain nose pliers
- Wire cutters
- Chasing hammer
- Bench block

To make the bracelet:

1 Follow the same process as for the Open Spiral Bracelet on page 24, except, after step 4, hold the spiral on the bench block and flatten it gently with the chasing hammer, being careful to hit just the spiral and not the straight part of the wire. Make three chains the length desired for the bracelet, less about ⅜", or the width of the clasp plus ⅛".

2 To attach the chains to the clasp, bend the first link in each chain open, slide one loop of the clasp onto a link, and bend the link closed. Repeat for the other two chains.

3 Make a jump ring by winding wire around the round nose pliers and then cutting through both ends of wire so you have a circle (Figure 1).

4 Make two more jump rings and attach the loose ends of the chains to the other end of the clasp.

Figure 1

To make the earrings:

1 Make one spiral as for the bracelet, except, instead of cutting the end after winding the straight wire around the round nose pliers, wrap the wire around itself, as shown (Figure 2).

2 Make another spiral, winding one extra time around to make it larger, then attaching it to the first.

3 Make a third by winding it two more times around than the first spiral and attaching it to the second spiral.

4 Open the loop on the ear wire and slide the loop on the small spiral into place and then close the loop on the ear wire.

5 Repeat for the other earring.

Figure 2

Copper and Swarovski Crystal Bracelet

FINISHED SIZE:
Approximately 8" long.

This project and the Gradations In Size Purple Bracelet (page 30) add a new dimension to a basic design, opening up the design possibilities to all the beads available, from semiprecious stones to the glittery Swarovski crystals. And you don't have to stop with just a bracelet. These projects, too, can be made into a necklace, earrings, and bracelet set. You are only limited by the hole size of your bead in relation to the size of your wire.

YOU WILL NEED

- 5 feet of 20-gauge soft copper wire
- 10 6mm peach Swarovski crystals
- Round nose pliers
- Chain nose pliers
- Wire cutters

1 Working from the spool, thread a crystal on the wire and bend the wire around the crystal (Figure 1). Note: If the wire is too stiff to bend around the crystal, bend the end at a 90-degree angle and make one spiral around the bend, slip the crystal in place, and continue.

Figure 1

2 Using the chain nose pliers, make a point in the spiral by grabbing the wire with the pliers as shown and continue to bend the wire around the spiral (Figure 2).

3 Make another wrap around the spiral, and then bend at a 90-degree angle, using round nose pliers (Figure 3).

Figure 2

4 Reposition the pliers and wrap the wire around the pliers, making a loop. Cut the excess wire close to the spiral (Figure 4).

5 As you make each new loop, slip on a previous link before step 4 (Figure 5).

Figure 3

6 Continue linking spirals until the chain is 8" long, or desired length less ½". Make a clasp as shown in the Basics section, pages 20-21. Open the loop on the first link, slide the clasp on, and close the loop.

Figure 4

Figure 5

Gradations in Size Purple Bracelet

A variation to the Copper and Swarovski Crystal Bracelet, this project opens up the possibilities of design. You can have the beads gradually increase in size as shown, or alternate small and large beads to create a different look. Your beads can be different colors from your wire or from each other. Just be sure to check before beginning this project that the beads you chose all slide easily onto your wire.

YOU WILL NEED

- 4 feet of 22-gauge soft purple craft wire
- One 6mm purple Swarovski crystal
- Six size 8 seed beads
- Two size 6 seed beads
- Round nose pliers
- Chain nose pliers
- Wire cutters

FINISHED SIZE:
Approximately 8" long.

1 Make four spirals the same as the Open Spiral Bracelet on page 24, linking them together as you make them (Figure 1).

Figure 1

2 Next, make three beaded spirals using the size 8 seed beads and following the directions for the Copper and Swarovski Crystal bracelet on page 29, linking them to the first three spirals (Figure 2).

3 Then make another beaded spiral with a size 6 bead, then one with the Swarovski crystal, one with the other size 6 bead, and three with the three remaining size 8 seed beads (Figure 3). Add enough open spirals to make the bracelet the desired length, less about ½".

Figure 2

4 Make a clasp following the instructions on pages 20-21 and add it to the first link in the chain.

Figure 3

Leaf Bracelet

This fun little bracelet is a variation that was inspired by the Leaf Box on page 78. The leaf design is easily adapted to links for the bracelet by adding the wrapped loop to link the elements together. This motif could also be used as the hanging chains for a mobile hanging in a window box, or to hang a sun catcher with a garden theme. Or, make one or two in sterling silver to accent beadwork flowers or a favorite lampwork bead, or to add to arrangements in Victorian beaded flowers.

YOU WILL NEED

- 4 feet of 20-gauge soft colored craft wire
- Round nose pliers
- Chain nose pliers
- Wire cutters

1 Begin making a spiral as for the Open Spiral Bracelet on page 24, through step 3, beginning with a loop a little smaller than ⅛".

2 Using the chain nose pliers, make a point in the wrap, as shown (Figure 1).

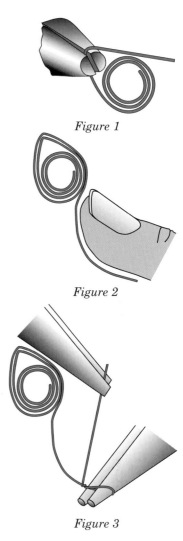

Figure 1

3 Wrap one more time around the spiral and then use your thumb to make a smooth curve away from the spiral (Figure 2).

4 Using the round nose pliers, grab the wire about ½" from the spiral and wrap it around the pliers, then twice around the wire (Figure 3).

Figure 2

5 Cut the wire about ½" from the wrap and make a small curl in the end with the round nose pliers.

6 Continue making leaves, sliding the last leaf made onto the wire before step 4 to link the elements together. As you do this, flip every other leaf over before sliding the previous one on, so they alternate direction. (See photo of finished bracelet on the facing page for guidance.)

7 Make the chain ½" shorter than desired. Then make a clasp, as shown on pages 20-21, adding it to the loop in first link before finishing the loop of the clasp.

Figure 3

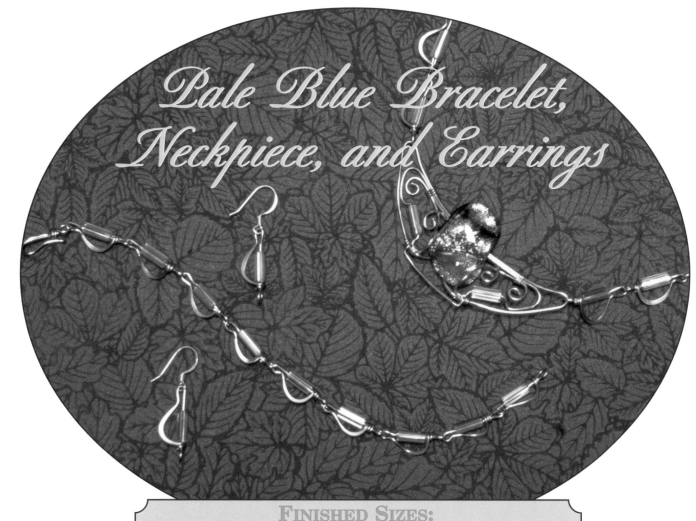

Pale Blue Bracelet, Neckpiece, and Earrings

FINISHED SIZES:
Bracelet, approximately 8" long; necklace, approximately 23" long; and earrings, approximately 1" long.

Here is a jewelry set that you can make either to showcase your favorite large bead (this one is fused glass), or to make in the chain design. Your beads determine the shape of the links, and the hammered loop accents the wire in the design.

YOU WILL NEED

- 12 feet of 20-gauge colored soft wire
- About 36 ½"-long beads
- One large accent bead
- One pair ear wires

- Round nose pliers
- Chain nose pliers
- Wire cutters
- Chasing hammer
- Bench block

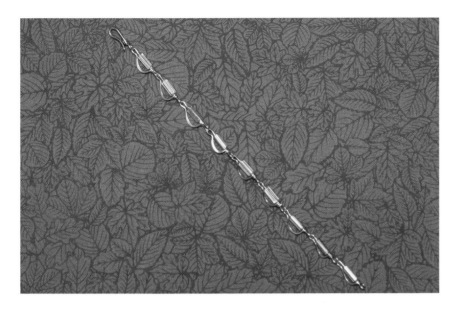

To make the bracelet:

1 Cut a 3" piece of wire. Grab the wire with the tip of the round nose pliers ⅛" from one end and bend to a 45-degree angle (Figure 1).

2 Grab the wire with the round nose pliers, just beyond the bend and wrap around the pliers, making a loop (Figure 2).

3 With the tip of the round nose pliers, grab just inside the loop and bend the long end of the wire parallel with the short end (Figure 3).

4 Thread a bead onto the long end of the wire. With the round nose pliers, grab the wire beyond the bead and bend the wire over the pliers (Figure 4).

5 With the tip of the round nose pliers, grab just beyond the bend, and pull the tail to a 45-degree angle. Using your fingers, bend the wire as shown in Figure 5.

Continued on next page

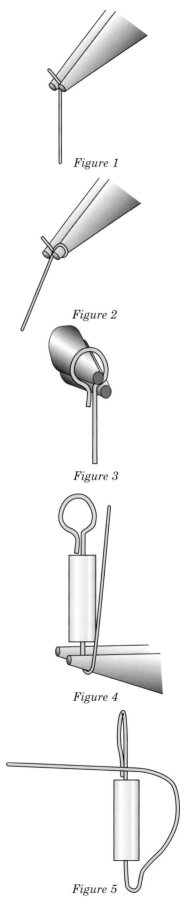

Figure 1

Figure 2

Figure 3

Figure 4

Figure 5

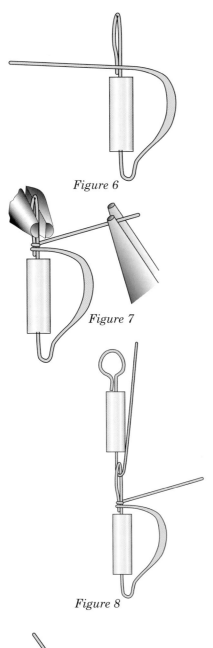

Figure 6

Figure 7

Figure 8

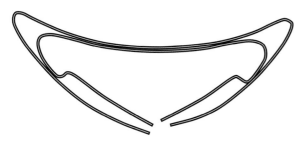

Figure 1

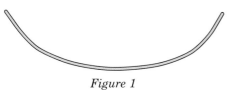

Figure 2

6 Pound the flap flat (Figure 6).

7 Grab the loop with the chain nose pliers and the tail with the round nose pliers. Wind the tail twice around the short tail and straight section close to the loop (Figure 7). Cut both tails close to the wrap.

8 Continue making links in the chain, sliding each previously made link onto the long wire before step 5, until the chain is ½" shorter than the desired size (Figure 8).

9 Make a clasp as shown on pages 20-21, sliding the first link in the loop of the clasp before wrapping around the wires.

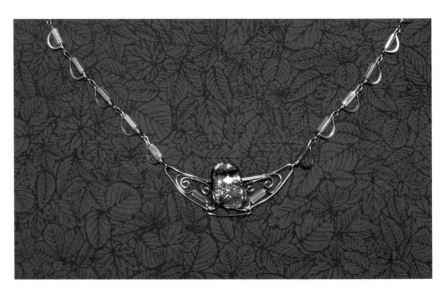

To make the neckpiece:

1 Cut two 10" lengths of wire, and with your hands, bend them into the gentle arch shown in Figure 1.

2 Thread the large bead onto the center of both wires.

3 Using the round nose pliers as well as your hands and following Figure 2, bend the wires as shown.

4 Thread a bead onto one wire and then bend as shown (Figure 3).

5 Cut four 2" pieces of wire and wrap the wires to hold them in place, as shown in Figure 4.

6 Bend one wire behind the large bead and one in front of it to hold it in place. Cut the tails of the wires ½" longer, then roll into loose spirals (Figure 5).

7 Cut a 3" piece of wire and wrap, as shown, below the large bead (Figure 6).

8 Make chains attached on either side of the neckpiece, following the directions for the bracelet, making to the desired length, minus ½".

9 Make a clasp the same as for the bracelet.

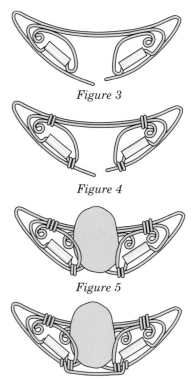

Figure 3

Figure 4

Figure 5

Figure 6

To make the earrings:

1 To make matching earrings, make a single link and slide it onto the loop of the ear wire.

2 Bend the loop closed.

3 Repeat for the other earring.

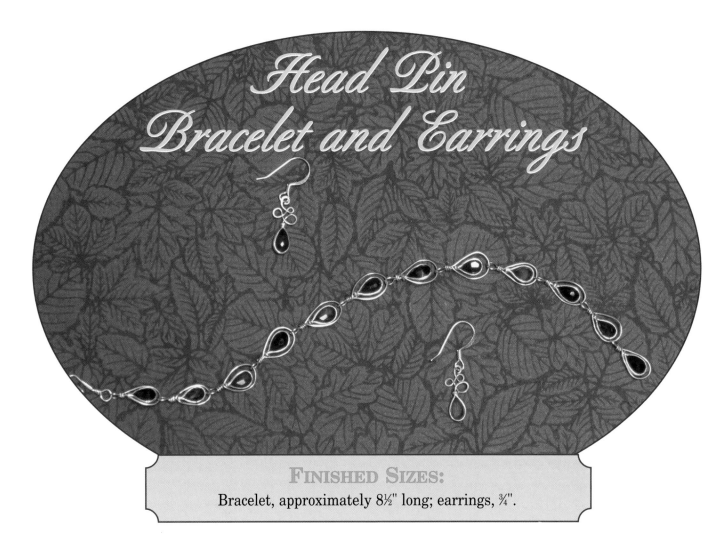

Head Pin Bracelet and Earrings

FINISHED SIZES:
Bracelet, approximately 8½" long; earrings, ¾".

Decorative head pins work into fabulous finished pieces. The design element on the head pin adds another dimension to your work, with soldered details and semiprecious stones that add elegance. Looping the wire around the stone in this bracelet creates the connection between the links as well as a nice detail in the design, and the earrings with their silver loops complement the bracelet pattern.

YOU WILL NEED

- 14 sterling silver 20- or 22-gauge 3½" head pins with oval or teardrop stones
- About 4" of 20- or 22-gauge sterling silver wire
- One pair of ear wires

- Round nose pliers
- Chain nose pliers
- Wire cutters
- Chasing hammer
- Bench block

To make the bracelet:

1 With the tip of the chain nose pliers, hold a head pin wire close to the stone, and bend the wire to a 45-degree angle (Figure 1).

2 With the round nose pliers, grab the wire just beyond the bend and wrap once around the pliers, making ⅛"-diameter circle (Figure 2).

3 With the tip of the round nose pliers, hold the wire just inside the loop and bend the tail parallel to the end at the stone end of the wire (Figure 3).

4 With the tip of the chain nose pliers, hold the wire as shown and bend up and around the stone, making the loop about ¹⁄₁₆" larger than the stone all the way around (Figure 4).

5 Grab the loop, as shown, with the chain nose pliers and grab the tail with the round nose pliers. Then, wrap the tail three times around the shank of the wire (Figure 5). Cut close to the wrap.

6 Make a total of 10 links in the bracelet, sliding the large loop around the stone of each previously made link into the small loop, before step 5.

7 Using the 4" of sterling silver wire, make a clasp as shown on pages 20-21, sliding the first link in the loop of the clasp before wrapping around the wires.

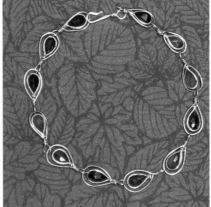

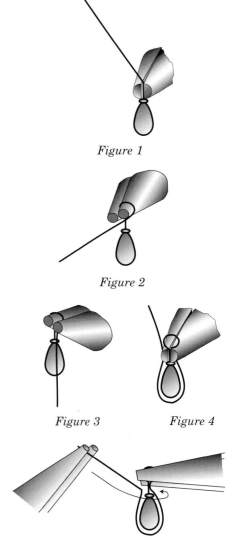

Figure 1

Figure 2

Figure 3   *Figure 4*

Figure 5

Tip

If you can't find decorative head pins at your bead store, you can make equally beautiful pieces by using plain head pins strung with one medium bead (about ¼" in diameter). This will also give you more flexibility in finding the color you want and for practice, since they will be less expensive.

Figure 1

Figure 2

To make the earrings:

1 With the round nose pliers, grab the head pin close to the stone and wrap once around the pliers (Figure 1).

2 Reposition the pliers as shown and wrap around the pliers in the opposite direction (Figure 2).

3 Repeat twice more, as shown, and cut close to the last loop (Figure 3).

4 Pound flatter at the top loop and just a little at the bottom loops.

5 Bend the ear wire loop open, slide the dangle onto the loop, and then close the loop.

6 Repeat the process for the other earring.

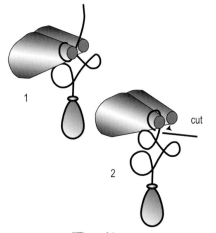

Figure 3

Head Pin Earrings Variation

FINISHED SIZE:
Approximately ¾" long.

Here, with just a few turns of wire and a little bit of hammering, you can create a beautiful earring design. This simple pattern takes the classic drop earring and gives it an added detail—creating a completely new design.

YOU WILL NEED

- Two sterling silver 20- or 22-gauge 3½" head pins with ⅜" long oval or teardrop stones
- One pair of ear wires
- Round nose pliers
- Chain nose pliers
- Chasing hammer
- Pounding block
- Wire cutters

1 Bend the head pin wire over to the right. Grab the wire about ¼" from the stone with the round nose pliers and bend around the pliers (Figure 1).

2 Grab the wire about ½" from the last bend and bend it the other way around the pliers (Figure 2).

3 Grab the wire about ¼" from the last bend and bend it halfway around the pliers (Figure 3).

4 Grab the wire about ¼" from the last bend and make a loop. Cut close to the loop (Figure 4).

5 Flatten the outer curves of the wire and attach to the ear wire.

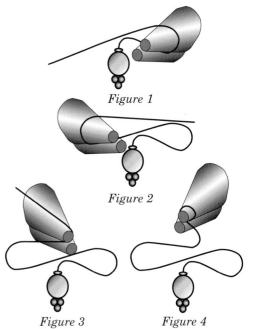

Figure 1

Figure 2

Figure 3   *Figure 4*

Head Pin Ring

FINISHED SIZE:
Ring size 6 to size 9, depending on placement of wraps.

This Victorian-styled ring is fun to make. You don't have to use it only as a ring, though. Flatten the circle a little, then slip a 1½" ribbon through it and place it on a hat, or make it larger and use it to hold a silk scarf around your neck.

The size of the ring is determined partly by where you make your wraps, and how much you curl the ends of the wire. So first measure your finger, then make sure that the distance between your two outer wraps is about ¼" to ½" less than the size of your finger.

YOU WILL NEED

- Two sterling silver 20- or 22-gauge 3½" head pins with oval, teardrop or diamond stones
- 4" of 20-gauge square wire
- 12" of 20-gauge half-round wire

- Round nose pliers
- Chain nose pliers
- Pin vise
- Wire cutters

1 Twist the square wire with the pin vise and trim ends to 3¼". Arrange the head pins and twisted wire as shown in Figure 1.

2 Make three wraps around the head pins with the half-round wire, holding the head pins and twisted wire with the chain nose pliers and winding the half-round wire with the round nose pliers. For each of the three wraps, be sure to wrap the wire three times around the pins. Cut close to the wraps. Press flat with the chain nose pliers.

3 Bend the head pin wires near the stones in opposite directions, as shown (Figure 2).

4 Bend the ring into a circle with the stones on top of the square wire ends (Figure 3). Adjust until it is the desired size.

5 Cut the ends of the head pin wires about ½" beyond the wraps and trim the square wire ends about ¾" beyond the wraps. Using the round nose pliers, curl the ends into spirals (Figure 4).

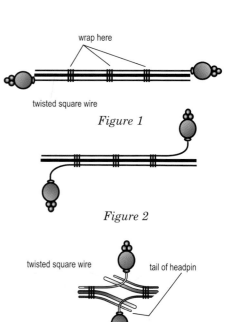

Figure 1

Figure 2

Figure 3

Figure 4

Head Pin Ring Variation

When making rings (and other projects, too), you are not limited to the design element at the end of your head pin. Here, a decorative bead is added to the design, giving the project a different look. With this simple trick, you can add new colors and textures to your ring that complement the head pin.

YOU WILL NEED

- Two sterling silver 20- or 22-gauge 3½" head pins with oval, teardrop or diamond stones
- 6" of 20-gauge square wire
- 12" of 20-gauge half-round wire

- Round nose pliers
- Chain nose pliers
- Pin vise
- Wire cutters

1 Make as for the Head Pin Ring on page 43, except, twist the 6" of wire, cut it to 5½", and use it in place of the 3¼" square wire in step 1.

2 Continue through step 4.

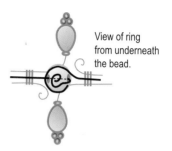

View of ring from underneath the bead.

3 Then, thread the bead on one end of the square wire, bending the wire so the bead is centered on the ring.

4 Cut the wires as in step 5, but curl the square wires as shown here (Figure 1).

Figure 1

Triangle Gems Bracelet and Earrings

FINISHED SIZES:
Bracelet, 8"; earrings, ¾".

I made this bracelet and earrings set for a good friend of mine for Christmas 2001. I was so happy with the finished gift that I made another with peridot stones for my sister, Joan, and I plan to make another for myself in aquamarine. A nice detail to the bracelet is that if the length is too long, you can just slip the clasp on the next link, and you will end up with a delicate little jeweled dangle from the extra link.

YOU WILL NEED

- 15 sterling silver 22-gauge 3½" head pins with small (about ¼" long) teardrop stones and silver filigree pattern
- One pair ear wires
- Round nose pliers
- Chain nose pliers
- Wire cutters

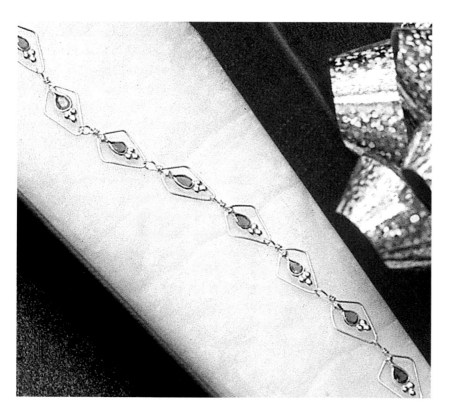

Figure 1

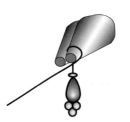

Figure 2

Figure 3

Figure 4

To make the bracelet:

1 With the tip of the chain nose pliers, hold a head pin wire close to the stone and bend the wire to a 45-degree angle (Figure 1).

2 With the round nose pliers, grab the wire just beyond the bend and wrap once around the pliers, making ⅛"-diameter circle (Figure 2).

3 With the tip of the round nose pliers, hold the wire just inside the loop and bend the tail parallel to the wire, as shown (Figure 3).

4 With the tip of the chain nose pliers, hold the wire as shown and bend to a 45-degree angle (Figure 4).

5 Hold the wire about ³⁄₁₆" away with the tip of the round nose pliers and bend it toward the tip of the head pin (Figure 5).

Continued on next page

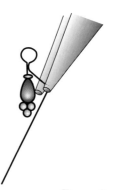

Figure 5

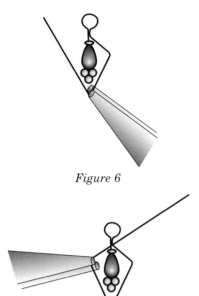

Figure 6

Figure 7

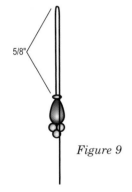

Figure 8

5/8"

Figure 9

6 Hold the wire a little less than ½" away and bend the end, as shown (Figure 6).

7 Hold the wire a bit less than ½" away and bend the end, as shown (Figure 7).

8 Hold the triangle and gem in your hand and wind the tail around the shank of the design (Figure 8). Repeat, making a total of 13 links, sliding the last link made onto the point of the one in progress just before winding the tail around the shank.

9 On the last link, instead of steps 1 through 3, bend the wire back onto itself ⅜" from the head pin detail (Figure 9). Finish the link through the rest of the steps, and then bend the folded end of wire into a hook.

To make the earrings:

1 Make one link as for the bracelet.

2 Bend the ear wire open, slide the link in place, and bend the ear wire closed.

3 Repeat for the other earring.

Green and Gold Circle Pin

FINISHED SIZE:
Approximately 1¼" circle.

Braiding with wire produces some wonderful effects. The colors of wire and the shiny properties of the enamel give a unique look to braidwork.

This design reminds me of a Celtic pattern. The flourish for the pin is an old design, most commonly seen as a decoration in calligraphy, which can become very ornate. This simple five-loop design is used for the head of the pin. It can also be used as a decorative element on a box or needlepoint, a Christmas ornament, or the top decoration for a sun catcher. You can continue adding more loops, and larger ones, and then gradually decrease, making the design as large as you choose.

This design element can be used for a variety of projects.

YOU WILL NEED

- 7½ feet of 22-gauge green-colored soft copper wire
- 3 feet of 22-gauge gold-colored soft copper wire
- 6" of 20-gauge gold-colored soft copper wire
- Round nose pliers
- Chain nose pliers
- Chasing hammer
- Bench block
- Wire cutters
- Small file
- A stationary device to weave around (I used a finishing nail, nailed into a work bench.)

To make the braid:

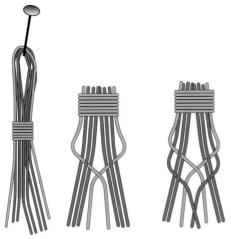

Figure 1 *Figure 2*

1 Cut three green wires and one gold wire to 30" lengths. Fold over the nail, arranging with the gold wire on the outside.

2 With the remaining gold wire, beginning 1" away from the nail, wrap tightly around the bundle of wires seven times (Figure 1). Cut close to the wrap.

3 Braid as shown in Figure 2 until the braid is 4¾" long. Wrap as at the beginning.

4 Cut the wires at one end to ½" from the wrap, and the wires at the other end to 1". Pound the wraps slightly with the chasing hammer.

5 Curl the braid into a circle, and then bend one end back on itself as shown (Figure 3). Curl the ends of the wires with round nose pliers.

1" tail wires 1/2" tail wires

Figure 3

To make the pin:

Figure 4

Figure 5

1 With the tip of the round nose pliers, grab the 20-guage wire 2½" from one end and bend to a 45-degree angle (Figure 4).

2 Grab ¼" away and bend to a 90-degree angle (Figure 5).

3 Grab ½" away, at ⅛" diameter on the pliers, and wind the wire around the pliers, as shown in Figure 6, winding under the wire.

4 Grab ½" away, at 1⁄16" diameter on the pliers, and wind in the opposite direction, over the wire (Figure 7).

5 Grab ¼" away at 1⁄16" diameter on the pliers, and wind in the same direction as step 4 (Figure 8).

6 Repeat step 5, passing over and then under the wire, as shown (Figure 9).

7 Repeat step 3, passing under and then over the wire, as shown (Figure 10).

8 Grab ½" away and bend to a 90-degree angle (Figure 11).

9 Grab as shown in Figure 12, wind twice around the wire, and cut.

10 Flatten the design with the chasing hammer and bench block. Lightly pound the length of the pin to harden the wire. File the tip of the pin to a smooth, rounded point.

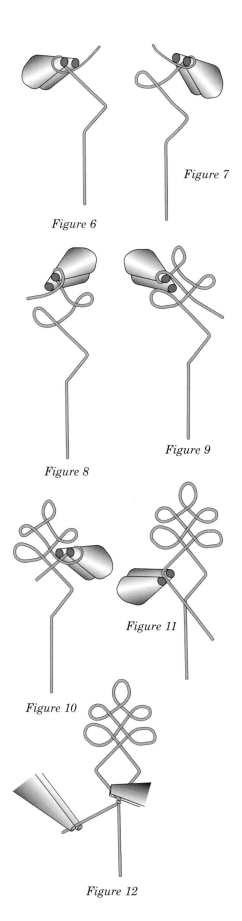

Figure 6

Figure 7

Figure 8

Figure 9

Figure 10

Figure 11

Figure 12

Bead Collection Pendant

FINISHED SIZE:
Approximately 1" x 3¼".

If you have some special beads that you love, but they have been tucked away in a drawer, here is an easy way to display them so you can enjoy them. The flourish at the top of the pendant is the same used for the Green and Gold Circle Pin, page 49.

YOU WILL NEED

- 10" of 20-gauge brass wire
- Various-sized beads with holes to fit the wire
- Ready-made chain 20" to 24"
- Round nose pliers

- Chain nose pliers
- Chasing hammer
- Bench block
- Wire cutters

1 Make the flourish, as for the pin in the Green and Gold Circle Pin on pages 50-51, starting each bend a little farther away than in the Circle Pin, and working a little farther down on the round nose pliers, so the finished scroll is larger.

2 String the beads onto the straight end of the wire.

3 Bend the end of the wire to a 45-degree angle and cut it to ⅜" from the last bead (Figure 1).

4 Grab the end of the wire with the round nose pliers and twist the end into a loop.

5 String your finished pendant on the ready-made chain.

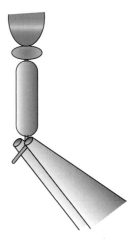

Figure 1

Treble Clef Earrings

Music is a big part of my family's life. From marching band, drum line, and concert band, to piano lessons, chamber music, and singing in a rock 'n' roll band, my family is entrenched. I just play with arts and crafts. So these earrings are a fun way to express my connection to the many facets of music around me. It is a fun and easy project that makes a great gift to a fellow music lover.

FINISHED SIZE:
Approximately ½" wide x 1¼" long.

YOU WILL NEED

- 10" of 18-gauge black-colored craft wire
- One pair ear wires
- Round nose pliers
- Chain nose pliers
- Wire cutters

1 Cut the wire in half.

2 Grab one end with the round nose pliers at ⅛" diameter of the pliers and wrap around the pliers (Figure 1).

3 Grab the wire 1¼" away and wind in the opposite direction (Figure 2).

4 With your hands, curve the wire behind, around, and over the tall straight section of the treble clef, making the large spiral (Figure 3). Cut excess wire.

5 Flatten the large curves slightly with the chasing hammer, and attach to the ear wires.

6 Repeat steps 2 through 5 for the other earring.

Figure 1

Figure 2

Figure 3

Basic Cage

FINISHED SIZE:
Approximately ¾" wide x 1½" long.

I first made cages with my son, Jeff, and some of his classmates for a school project. Each student was to study some aspect of the Renaissance. They could then make something related to their studies to sell at a schoolwide Renaissance Faire. Students chose things like foods of the times and brought fresh baked breads, or daily life and brought flowered hair wreaths.

But alas, my son wanted to read about the plague…. I figured he wouldn't be selling anything at the fair. However, Jeff came across information that doctors of the times would make and sell "magic" amulets made of different stones to ward off disease, and so I helped him and his group make a bunch of "magic" amulets, which were a hit with the kids and sold out at the fair.

YOU WILL NEED

- About 30" of 20- or 22-gauge soft copper wire
- One glass pebble
- Round nose pliers
- Chain nose pliers
- Wire cutters

1 Cut four 5" lengths of wire. Arrange the four wires as shown and make three wraps around them, winding the wire with the round nose pliers. Make each wrap three or four times around. Cut close to the wraps. Press flat with the chain nose pliers (Figure 1).

2 With your hands, curve the wire around the glass pebble (Figure 2).

3 Remove the glass and bend the wires parallel to each other with the flat nose pliers (Figure 3).

4 Wrap tightly around all the wires, four or five times around (Figure 4).

5 Fit the glass pebble into the circle and bend the top wire in toward the center between the wraps as shown in Figure 5.

6 Turn the piece over and bend the back wires in toward the center, encasing the glass in the wire cage.

7 Use one of the top wires to make a loop, wrapping the end several times around the base of the loop. Cut close to the wrap. Curl the rest of the top wires into open spirals with the round nose pliers.

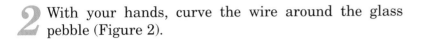

Figure 1

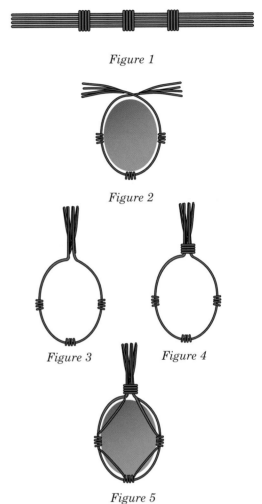

Figure 2

Figure 3

Figure 4

Figure 5

Tip

Made from the glass pebbles used at the bottom of fish bowls or vases, these quick little pieces make great sun catchers, baubles at the end of a drawstring purse, or just fun necklaces for kids to wear. They are also good practice for wirework, though a bit challenging, I found, as a first project for seventh-graders.

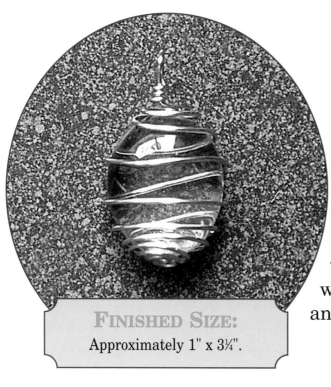

Spiral Cage

This is the easiest cage to make and can be used for just about any shaped object, making it a great way to hold freeform stones or beads. A variation that some of the kids used was to just randomly wrap wire around the glass, without any particular pattern at all.

YOU WILL NEED

- About 12" of 20- or 22-gauge colored craft wire
- One glass pebble
- Round nose pliers
- Chain nose pliers
- Wire cutters

Figure 1

Figure 2

Figure 3

1 Make a tight spiral as shown on page 19, winding until the spiral is about ¼" in diameter.

2 Continue winding two more times around, making a looser spiral, so the wire doesn't touch itself (Figure 1).

3 Push the glass pebble into the center of the spiral and begin winding the wire around the glass, following the shape of the glass (Figure 2).

4 When you reach the top of the glass, use the tip of the round nose pliers to bend the wire to a 90-degree angle from the glass (Figure 3).

5 Make a loop with the tail and wrap the tail two or three times around the base of the loop. Cut close to the wrap.

Claw Cage

This cage is easier to complete than the Basic Cage, though a little more complex than the Spiral Cage. It is my favorite because it leaves the center open and is easy to make, after a little practice. The size of the zigzag you make with the wire, along with the thickness of the glass pebble, determine how much the "claws" curve to the front and back of the finished piece.

FINISHED SIZE:
Approximately ¾" wide x 1¼" long.

YOU WILL NEED

- About 12" of 20- or 22-gauge colored craft wire
- One glass pebble
- Round nose pliers
- Chain nose pliers
- Flat nose pliers
- Wire cutters

1 Make a loop with ⅛" shank, as shown (Figure 1).

2 Using the round nose pliers, make zigzags, with the first and last folds being ¼" and all the rest ½" (Figure 2).

3 Bend the zigzag into a circle. Grab with the chain nose pliers and wind three times around the shank of the loop (Figure 3). Cut close to the wind.

4 With the flat nose pliers, bend the curves of the zigzags in to the center of the circle (Figure 4).

5 Place the glass in the circle and bend the other side of the zigzags towards the center, adjusting the wire so the glass fits snugly inside the cage.

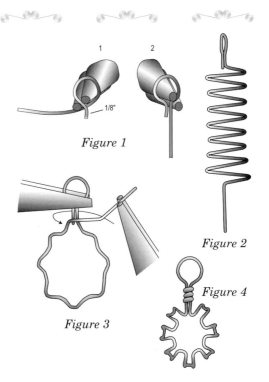

Figure 1

Figure 2

Figure 3

Figure 4

Section 3:
Projects for Your Home and Your Favorite Things

Bead-Fringed Lampshade

I love this little lamp with its dangling green fringe. It reminds me of some friends who collected antiques and had a large hanging Victorian lamp over their dining room table that was dripping with beaded fringe in rich blues. My little green version sits on my computer so I can occasionally daydream of moss-covered forests with ferns and tall trees....

This project, like the linked bracelets, is a good one for practicing wirework.

You Will Need

- 6"-diameter lampshade
- ½-yard of fabric
- ⅞-yard of gimp with loops the jump rings can fit through
- 127 jump rings
- 42 2½" eye pins
- 43 2" head pins
- 42 leaf beads
- 85 oval beads
- 85 light green size 6 beads
- 170 size 5 green triangle beads
- About 28 grams of size 8 green seed beads
- Round nose pliers
- Chain nose pliers
- Wire cutters
- Craft glue
- Pencil
- Scissors

To cover the shade:

1 Press the fabric, wrong side up. Lay the lampshade on the fabric at the seam of the shade and mark about ¼" beyond the shade at the top and bottom.

2 Slowly roll the shade on the fabric, marking the outside dimensions every inch or so on the fabric until you reach the seam of the shade again. Mark 1" beyond the seam. Cut along the pencil lines (Figure 1).

3 Spread craft glue along the top and bottom edge, as well as the seam of the lampshade, and press the fabric in place. Let dry.

4 Cut off the excess fabric, leaving a ¼" overlap at the seam. Use a small amount of glue to carefully glue the raw edge of the overlap in place.

5 Glue the gimp around the top of the shade.

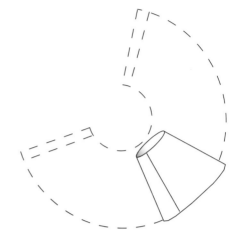

Figure 1

To make the fringe:

1 Open the jump rings and slide them into the remaining gimp all along one side, passing through the loop in the gimp. Measure around the shade to make sure 85 loops are enough to fit around. Adjust, if necessary. Set aside.

2 To prepare the leaf ends and make the long dangles ("A" and "B" in Figure 2), open a jump ring and slide an eye pin onto it, followed by a glass leaf. Close the jump ring. Repeat for a total of 42 leaves. Thread 14 of them with Pattern A and 28 with Pattern B, cutting each one ⅜" beyond the last bead and using the round nose pliers to bend the end into a loop.

3 Thread 28 head pins as in Pattern C and 15 as in Pattern D, cutting each one to ⅜" beyond the last bead and making a loop as in step 2.

4 Beginning with the first jump ring on the gimp, slide a dangle on the jump ring, and then close the ring. Repeat the following pattern order: D, C, B, A, B, C. The last dangle will be Pattern D again.

5 Put a thin line of glue along the bottom of the shade and attach the bead-fringed gimp while the shade is resting on a table with the beaded fringe fanning out in the circle around the shade. Let dry thoroughly before picking up the shade.

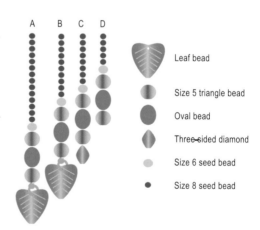

A	B	C	D

Leaf bead

Size 5 triangle bead

Oval bead

Three-sided diamond

Size 6 seed bead

Size 8 seed bead

Figure 2

Fringed Tea Light Candleholder

FINISHED SIZE:
Approximagely 3½" tall x 3½" wide.

I like making this candleholder because it's like making something from nothing, since you create the structure to hold the tea light candle as well as the bead curtain that hangs in front of the flame. It doesn't really matter what shape beads you use, but try to choose beads that are transparent or translucent so the candlelight shines through.

YOU WILL NEED

- 4½ feet of 16-gauge colored craft wire
- 4 feet of 20-gauge colored craft wire
- One spool of 24-gauge soft copper wire in a color to match beads
- 42 2½" eye pins
- 43 2" head pins
- Assortment of beads (transparent or translucent with hole large enough for 20-gauge wire)
- Round nose pliers
- Chain nose pliers
- Wire cutters

1 Cut three 14" lengths of the 16-gauge wire. Bend each length to right angles, 5¼" from each end (Figure 1).

2 Using the 20-gauge wire and chain nose pliers, wrap the wires together at the bend, forming a triangle (Figure 2).

3 Working with each pair of end wires one at a time, bend them into a diamond shape near the wrap, then twist them together to 1" from the ends (Figure 3). Curl the ends up. Repeat for the other two pairs, and then adjust the structure so that the top is level and all the legs touch the table.

4 Use the remaining 16-gauge wire to make the tea light holder, making three arms as shown in Figure 4, then bending them up ½" from each end.

Continued on next page

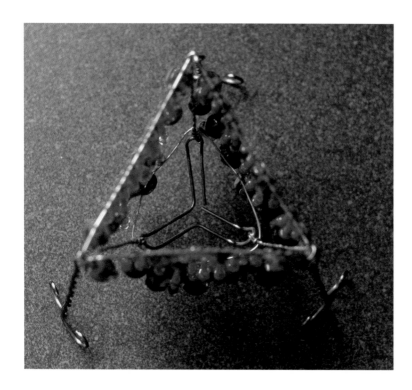

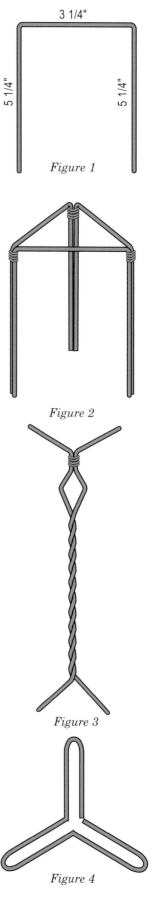

3 1/4"

5 1/4"   5 1/4"

Figure 1

Figure 2

Figure 3

Figure 4

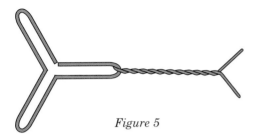

Figure 5

5 Cut three 6" lengths of 20-gauge wire and fold one in half over the corner of the triangle structure. Then twist the wire ends together for 2" (Figure 5).

6 Cut where the 2"-twist ends, and with the round nose pliers, curl the end of the twisted 20-gauge wire around one of the arms of the tea light holder (Figure 6).

7 Repeat with the other two corners of the triangle and tea light holder.

8 Cut an 8" length of 20-gauge wire and wrap it around the twisted 20-gauge wire from step 5 near the tea light holder (Figure 7). Adjust this wire so a tea light can fit inside the circle of wire.

Figure 6

To make the fringe:

1 Working from the spool of the 24-gauge wire, string the bead for the end of the dangle and twist the wire together close to the bead (Figure 8).

2 Cut the wire ½" longer than the dangle will be and string the rest of the beads.

3 Wrap the remaining wire around one of the triangle's wires four times and cut close to the wrap (Figure 9).

4 Repeat for each dangle, making the dangles about 1½" long at the sides, and up to 2½" in the middle.

Figure 7

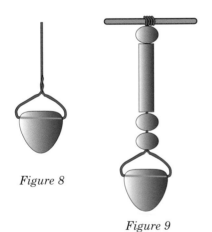

Figure 8

Figure 9

Brown Spiral Box Lid

FINISHED SIZE:
Lid diameter approximately 1¾" to fit a 2" box.

This simple, quick lid can easily be made for different-sized jars, just by winding the spiral more or fewer times around. You can also make it a dome-shaped lid by pulling the finished lid up in the center. It will always have a little spring to it, something my children never tire of playing with.

YOU WILL NEED

- 5 feet of 16-gauge colored craft wire
- Small 2"-diameter round box with indented rim

- Round nose pliers
- Chain nose pliers
- Wire cutters

Figure 1

Figure 2

Figure 3

Figure 4

1 Cut an 8" length of wire and bend it around the rim of the box. Bend up the ends so that they are about ½" away from each other and then make a loop in each end (Figure 1).

2 Using the remaining wire, make a ½" open spiral. This will be the handle of the lid.

3 Grab the wire at the base of the spiral and begin another spiral, perpendicular to the first spiral (Figure 2).

4 Continue spiraling tightly around until the spiral is the diameter of the box opening. Thread the end through the two loops on the box and bend it back toward the first loop (Figure 3).

5 Cut the wire 1" from the bend.

6 Open the first loop on the box and slide the end of the 1" wire in the loop. Close the loop (Figure 4).

7 Make a loop at the end of the 1" of wire. Adjust the angle of the loops on the box, if necessary, so the lid opens and closes easily.

Red Woven Lid on Glass Jar

With its snug-fitting lid, I don't need to worry if this jar is knocked over by roaming cats or hanging sleeves. The beads stay safe in the jar with its brightly colored lid, and I can color-coordinate the contents of each jar I make!

YOU WILL NEED

- 5 feet of 18-gauge colored craft wire
- One spool of 24-gauge colored craft wire
- Small 2"-diameter glass jar with indented rim
- ⅛"-diameter stick or wire

- Round nose pliers
- Chain nose pliers
- Wire cutters
- Awl

Figure 1

Figure 2

Figure 3

Figure 4

1 Using the 18-gauge wire, make a ⅜" open spiral.

2 Begin another spiral, perpendicular to the first and winding counterclockwise (or clockwise if you are left-handed).

3 Cut a 4-foot length of 24-gauge wire and begin winding it closely around the wire of the second spiral, holding a small tail to keep the wire taut (Figure 1).

4 Continue winding the 24-gauge wire around the 18-gauge wire as you spiral the 18-gauge wire. When you have made the first circle, wrap the 24-gauge wire once through two rounds of the 18-gauge wire (a long stitch) (Figure 2). Repeat this about every ⅛" along the 18-gauge wire for the second round.

5 Every round after that, thread through the previous round just before the same long stitch (Figure 3). Don't wrap the 18-gauge wire too tightly, or you won't be able to thread the 24-gauge wire through the previous round of 18-gauge wire. Use an awl to press an opening between the wires to fit the 24-gauge wire through.

6 When the 24-gauge wire is about 2½" long, cut a new length of wire and begin wrapping it around, holding a 2" or 3" tail to help keep the wraps tight. Cut the tails close to the inside of the lid after you have worked for at least ½". Continue until the lid is the size of the jar opening.

7 Make a clasp by making a long stitch. Then, using the round nose pliers to bend the 18-gauge wire into a ¾" loop, make another long stitch and continue winding the 24-gauge wire as before until you reach the side opposite the clasp, less ¼" (Figure 4).

To make the hinge:

1 Make a long stitch and then wind the 18-gauge wire three times around the ⅛"-diameter stick or wire (Figure 5).

2 Make two more long stitches anchoring the 18-gauge wire back to the lid, and then wrap the 18-gauge wire three more times around the stick or wire. Make sure you will be able to slide the stick or wire out of the winding.

3 Cut the 18-gauge wire at an angle about ⅜" from the hinge (Figure 6).

4 Anchor the 18-gauge wire to the lid with a long stitch and then wind the 24-gauge wire around the 18-gauge wire to the cut mark.

5 Finish with enough long stitches to cover the end of the 18-gauge wire and two more times to anchor the 24-gauge wire (Figure 7). Cut the 24-gauge wire close to the bottom of the lid.

6 Cut a piece of 18-gauge wire the circumference of the jar rim plus 2". Bend the wire so it fits around the jar rim. (You will need to make it a little smaller than the rim so it hugs the rim.)

7 Bend the ends up so they are about ¾" apart. Then bend the ends toward each other so they cross over one another (Figure 8).

8 Thread these ends through the hinge in the lid. Fit the 18-gauge wire on the rim of the jar, cut the ends to ¼" beyond the hinges, and bend the ends around the hinges (Figure 9).

9 Tighten the fit of the 18-gauge wire around the rim by bending the ¾" space by the hinge. Bend the clasp as shown (Figure 10).

Figure 5

Figure 6

Figure 7

Figure 8

Figure 9

Figure 10

Black and Gold Thimble Basket

Here's the perfect-sized basket to hold your thimble when taking a break from quilting. Hang it on a hook near where you quilt, and you'll always know where to find your favorite finger protector.

YOU WILL NEED

- 5 feet of 18-gauge black-colored craft wire
- One spool of 28-gauge gold-colored craft wire
- Round nose pliers
- Wire cutters

1 Beginning at the bottom of the basket and using the round nose pliers, make a small spiral with the black wire, winding two loose rounds counterclockwise (or clockwise if you are left-handed) (Figure 1).

Figure 1

2 Cut a 4-foot length of gold wire. Wrap the wire once around both rounds (a long stitch) and then once around the current round, leaving about 1⁄16" of space between each wrap, so the black wire shows (Figure 2).

Figure 2

3 Continue the pattern of step 2 around until you have eight of the long wraps, or long stitches (Figure 3).

Figure 3

4 Now make each long stitch just after every short stitch of the previous round. Then make a wrap around the current round (a short wrap), always spiraling the black wire loosely so you can thread the 28-gauge wire easily through the previous rounds (Figure 4).

Figure 4

5 When the spiral is almost 1" in diameter, begin spiraling up to make the sides of the basket.

6 On the eighth round on the side of the basket, make four short wraps, instead of one, and continue this pattern for four rounds total (Figure 5).

Round 8

Figure 5

7 On the last round, make five short wraps, followed by one long stitch all the way around (Figure 6).

8 When you reach the beginning of the round, loop the black wire into a 3⁄4" ring (for hanging the basket), cut it about 3⁄8" beyond the loop, and continue the long and short wraps and stitches until the wire is covered to the end (Figure 7).

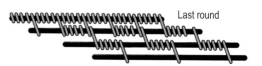

Last round

Figure 6

9 Pull the tail of the gold wire through to the inside of the basket and cut it close to the basket.

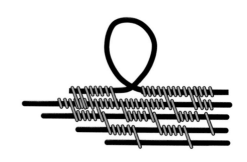

Figure 7

Miniature Gold Basket

Just the right size for a ring or pair of earrings, this little basket is right at home on a knickknack shelf or can become a nice holder for a small little gift.

YOU WILL NEED

- One spool of 20-gauge craft wire
- One spool of 28-gauge craft wire
- Round nose pliers
- Wire cutters
- Awl

Beginning at the bottom of the basket:

1 Cut six 4" lengths of 20-gauge wire.

2 Hold three of the wires together, and working from the spool, begin wrapping the 28-gauge wire tightly around the center of the three wires, six times around (Figure 1).

3 Center the other three wires over the wrapping of the first three and begin winding the 28-gauge wire over and under the sets of wire, six times around (Figure 2).

4 Now spread the wires evenly and begin winding over and under each wire four times around. Then skip one wire and follow the same winding pattern four times around before skipping one wire again (Figure 3 and Figure 4). Continue until the bottom of the basket is about 1" in diameter.

5 Bend all the 20-gauge wires perpendicular to the bottom of the basket and continue the same pattern up the sides of the basket.

6 When the sides of the basket are ⅜" tall, wrap the 28-gauge wire twice around one of the 20-gauge wires and cut. Cut the four 20-gauge wires shown to ½" beyond the basket top and the rest to ¼" beyond the top.

7 Loop the short wires over the last row of weaving, spiral two of the long wires for the front of the basket, and make loops in the remaining long wires for the hinge to the basket lid (Figure 5).

8 Begin the lid the same as the basket bottom through step 4. Wind the 28-gauge wire twice around one of the 20-gauge wires and cut close to the wrap.

9 Bend each 20-gauge wire around the 20-gauge wire next to it (Figure 6).

10 Loop two of the 20-gauge wires around the hinge loops on the basket and spiral the 20-gauge wire opposite for a clasp (Figure 7). Cut the rest close to the basket.

11 Use the awl to make a small space in the top of the lid, just enough to slide a 2" piece of 20-gauge wire through.

12 Spiral the wire as shown to make the handle (Figure 8).

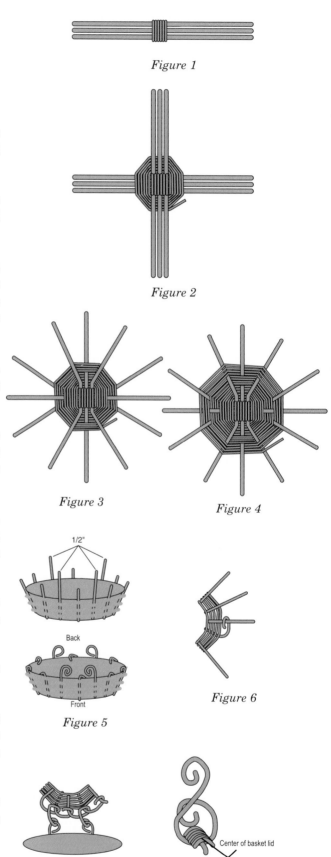

Figure 1

Figure 2

Figure 3

Figure 4

Figure 5

Figure 6

Figure 7

Figure 8

Woven Handle on Wood Jar Lid

FINISHED SIZE:
Approximately ¾" wide x 2" tall handle.

This simple addition to a ready-made lid on a glass jar is an example of why I like wirework so much. You can make so many utilitarian—yet beautiful—things with wire. Here, the braided wire handle makes the lid easier to pick up, and at the same time, adds a decorative detail to an otherwise plain jar

YOU WILL NEED

- 40" of 20-gauge soft brass-colored wire
- 3 feet of 24-gauge soft brass-colored wire
- 2 feet of 24-gauge soft copper-colored wire
- Wooden lidded jar
- Round nose pliers
- Chain nose pliers
- Pin vise
- Wire cutters
- Drill
- Glue
- Clamp

1 Cut 12" of the 24-gauge brass-colored wire and set it aside.

2 Use the pin vise and chain nose pliers to twist the 2 feet of copper-colored wire and 2 feet of 24-gauge brass-colored wire together.

3 Cut the 20-gauge wire into four 10" lengths and the twisted wire into two 10" lengths.

4 Group the wires, as shown, and bend into two loops at the center (Figure 1). Use a clamp to hold the wires in place.

5 Carefully weave, as shown, keeping the wires parallel to each other in each group of three (Figure 2).

6 When the braid is the desired length, twist the two center sets of wire tightly together and cut ½" long (Figure 3).

7 Cut the outer sets of wire ⅛" beyond the last braid and bend them over the braid (Figure 4).

8 Unclamp the top folds of the braid and wrap five times around them with the 12" of 24-gauge brass-colored wire.

9 Drill a hole in the wood lid the width of the twisted bottom of the braid and glue the braid in the hole.

Figure 1

Figure 2

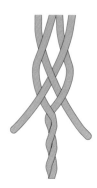

Figure 3

Figure 4

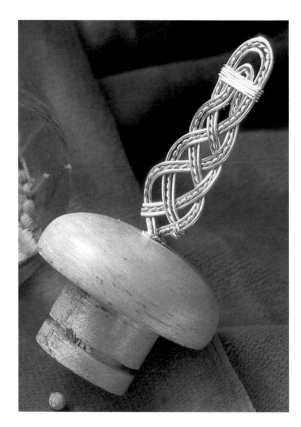

Green Leaf Box

Finished Size:
2" wide x 2" tall.

As you may have noticed, I like decorating small containers. This little green one is the first of a trio of little wooden "pumpkin boxes" I have been finding ways to decorate for years. Here, graceful leaves and lines of wire wind around the box.

You Will Need

- Small wooden box, painted and varnished
- One spool of 20- or 22-gauge colored wire
- Round nose pliers
- Chain nose pliers
- Super Glue®
- Toothpicks

1. Working from the spool, put a drop of glue on the rim of the box and glue the end of the wire against the rim, holding it in place with a toothpick until it is dry.

2. Wind the wire three times around the rim of the box, and then spiral it around the center of the box (Figure 1).

3. Cut the wire about ⅛" from the rim, drip glue over the wire in a few spots, and hold it in place with the toothpick until dry.

4. With a new length of wire, glue three rounds of wire to the bottom rim the same way you began at the top. Cut and glue in place.

Figure 1

To make individual leaves:

1. Begin making a spiral as for the Open Spiral Bracelet on page 24, through step 3, beginning with a loop a little smaller than ⅛".

2. Using the chain nose pliers, make a point in the wrap, as shown (Figure 2).

3. Wrap one more time around the spiral and then use your thumb to make a smooth curve away from the spiral (Figure 3).

4. Bend the tail back toward the leaf and cutting it about ⅜" from the bend. Make a small curl in the end (Figure 4).

5. Use the pliers and your hands to curve the leaves to fit the shape of the box. Place one leaf at a time on the box and drip glue on the wire so it seeps under and adheres the leaf in place. Hold the leaf with a toothpick until the glue hardens. Repeat until you've covered the box.

6. Glue two or three leaves to the box lid.

Figure 2

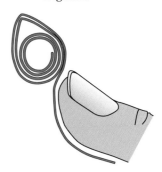

Figure 3

Figure 4

Pale Blue Spiral Box

FINISHED SIZE:
2" wide x 2" tall with lid.

Second in this trio of little wooden boxes is a sky blue and white box, covered in spirals, large and small. This is a fun box to make and provides the opportunity to practice different types and sizes of spirals.

YOU WILL NEED

- Small wooden box, painted and varnished
- One spool of 20- or 22-gauge colored wire
- Round nose pliers
- Chain nose pliers
- Super Glue®
- Toothpicks

1 Begin the same as in the Green Leaf Box project, page 79, except wind the wire about six more times around the rim.

2 Then cut the wire 2" long and make a large spiral (Figure 1). Use the pliers to bend the spiral to the shape of the box and glue it in place.

3 Turn the box over and repeat for the bottom rim.

4 Make large and small spirals, curving them to the shape of the box and then gluing them in place.

5 Begin a spiral around the handle on the lid of the box, spiral it out on the surface of the lid, and cut. Glue in place.

6 Glue two more spirals with long tails to the lid.

Figure 1

Pink Hearts Box

FINISHED SIZE:
2" wide x 2" tall with lid.

Valentine's Day always comes to mind when I think of the dancing hearts on this little pink box. The third of the trio of "pumpkin boxes," this one is so easy to finish, and it could hold anything from a single chocolate to a nice piece of jewelry.

YOU WILL NEED

- Small wooden box, painted and varnished
- Varied sizes of colored wire
- Round nose pliers
- Chain nose pliers
- Super Glue®
- Toothpicks
- Chasing hammer
- Bench block

To make a heart shape:

1 Cut a 2" length of wire.

2 With the tip of the round nose pliers, bend the wire into a V-shape.

3 Pinch the point of the "V" slightly (Figure 1).

4 Spiral each end in towards the center, creating a heart shape (Figure 2).

5 Make large and small hearts from different thickness and colors of wire. Pound some flat and leave some round.

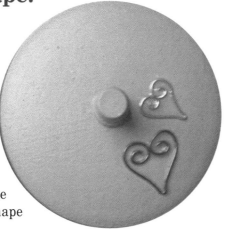

Figure 1

Figure 2

To glue in place:

1 Bend the wire shape gently to fit the curve of the box.

2 Hold in place with a toothpick and drip the Super Glue onto the wire so it seeps onto the box and glues the wirework in place.

3 Repeat for each element, placing hearts randomly on the box and lid.

Andrew's Hanging Hearts

FINISHED SIZE:
1½" wide x 2½" long.

O ne day, my son, Andrew, wanted to play with some wire. He took our wirework box into his room and after a quiet time of experimentation, he emerged with these hanging hearts for me. Surprises like this "just because" gift are memories of my parenthood that I will cherish all my life. And besides that, it was a pretty cool design, too!

YOU WILL NEED

- 2 feet of 20-gauge red colored craft wire
- Round nose pliers
- Chain nose pliers
- Wire cutters

1 Fold the wire in half at the center, pinching it with the pliers so it forms a point.

2 With your hands, arch the wire around to a heart shape (Figure 1).

3 With the chain nose pliers, grab the wire where the ends overlap and twist the ends together for about 1" (Figure 2).

4 Fold the twisted part of the wire up, adjusting the heart shape if necessary (Figure 3).

5 Cut the wire ends 1½" from the twist. Bend one end into a small heart shape and wrap the other end around the base of the small heart (Figure 4).

Figure 1

Figure 2

Figure 3

My version of Andrew's hearts.

Figure 4

Fern on Black Box Inset

This elegant fern pattern reminds me of morning walks in the forest with footsteps on pine needles and mushrooms growing under ferns. It would be as easily at home made into a lapel pin or as an accent on a needlework project.

FINISHED SIZE:
Leaf motif, approximately 1¾" wide x 2" high.

YOU WILL NEED

- 3" of 16-gauge green craft wire
- 2 feet of 24-gauge green craft wire
- One spool of 28-gauge green craft wire
- Small piece of suede cut to the size of the lid opening

- Thread to match suede
- Sewing needle
- Round nose pliers
- Chain nose pliers
- Wire cutters

1 Cut the 24-gauge wire in half.

2 Hold the 16-gauge and two 24-gauge wires together and wind 28-gauge wire around them for ½", keeping the 16-gauge wire in the center of the two 24-gauge wires (Figure 1).

3 Bend the 24-gauge wires into a leaf shape, making the smooth arch of the leaf with your fingers and the point and base of the leaf with the tip of the round nose pliers (Figure 2).

4 Wind the 28-gauge wire around the three wires again for about ⅜" and then make two more leaves, smaller than the first (Figure 3).

5 Bend the wrapped wire into a slight curve, then continue, making smaller and smaller leaves and wrapping the wires, shaping the stem of the growing fern as you go.

6 When the leaves become so small that they are just loops, stop making them on the inside curve of the fern and just make a few more on the outside curve (Figure 4).

7 Wind around the three wires several more times and cut the 24-gauge wires.

8 Wind loosely around the 16-gauge wire for about ¾". Cut the 28-gauge wire and trim the 16-gauge wire, if necessary. Use the round nose pliers to curl the end of the 16-gauge wire into a spiral for the tip of the fern (Figure 5).

9 Stitch the wire fern onto a piece of suede and fit it into the box opening.

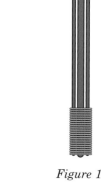

Figure 1

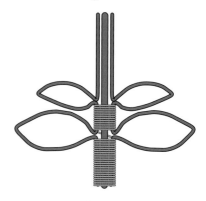

Figure 2

Figure 3

Figure 4

Figure 5

Hexagon Box

Here is an easy, versatile way to dress up a plain cardboard box with colored wire.

The trick to threading wire through the holes is to make sure the wire doesn't kink as you pull it through. If you keep the wire in a smooth loop, it will slide through easily.

You can adapt this design to different sizes of boxes by enlarging or reducing the pattern on the copier. You can also vary the design by passing the wire from the inner ring to the outer ring at different distances, by weaving in and out of the finished design, or by adding beads.

YOU WILL NEED

- 3" cardboard box with lid, painted
- 9 feet of 24-gauge colored craft wire
- Needle (at least as thick as the wire)
- Pair of utility pliers to hold the needle (the kind with the ridges)
- Paper and pencil to copy the dot pattern (or use photocopier)

1 Photocopy or trace the dot pattern onto a sheet of paper (Figure 1).

2 Center the paper over the lid of the cardboard box and tape in place.

3 Using the pliers to hold the needle, poke holes through the paper and lid at every dot.

4 Cut a 7-foot length of wire and thread from the inside of the lid up through one of the center ring's holes, leaving a 6" tail to hold onto as you make the first few stitches.

5 Pass down through the hole in the outer ring that is five holes away from the hole directly opposite the hole the wire is coming up through (Figure 2).

6 Pull the wire firmly and press flat against the lid. Pass the wire up through the next hole on the center ring and then down the next hole on the outer ring (Figure 3). Continue in this manner around the box until you have all the holes filled.

7 On the inside of the lid, twist the wire ends tightly together, cut about ⅛" from the lid, and fold over and press against the lid so the twisted wires are not sticking out.

8 Cut a 2-foot length of wire and thread an end through one of the outer holes.

9 Loop around each wire as shown in Figure 4, all the way around the box. Then pass the wire back down the first hole and twist and cut the wires as in step 7.

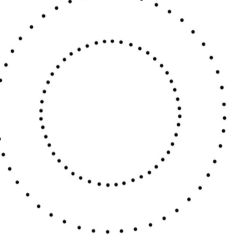

Figure 1

Figure 2

Figure 3

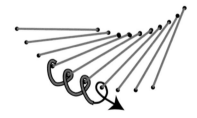

Figure 4

Fleur-de-lis on Mesh Box and as Charm on Needlepoint

FINISHED SIZE:
Fleur-de-lis on box, ¾" wide x 1" tall; fleur-de-lis charm, approximately 1¼" wide by 1½" tall.

The fleur-de-lis is an old symbol, which is the stylized shape of a white iris. It is most well-known for being the symbol of France from the 12th century on, and more recently, it has become the symbol of the Boy Scouts. I think it is a beautiful form and a design element that I like to use often. This little emblem on the mesh box adds a little touch of detail and ties in nicely with the brass-colored clasp. And a larger fleur-de-lis, pounded flat on its long curves, is a wonderful accent to the soft textures of yarn in needlepoint.

YOU WILL NEED (BOTH PROJECTS)

- Box with mesh lid at least 1" x 1¼"
- 12" of 22-gauge craft wire for gold charm
- 2 feet of 16-gauge craft wire for silver charm
- Round nose pliers
- Chain nose pliers
- Wire cutters
- Chasing hammer
- Bench block

To make mesh box project:

1 Cut 4" from the 22-gauge wire and set aside for wrapping.

2 Fold the remaining wire in half.

3 With the tip of the round nose pliers, grab one side of the wire 1" from the fold. Bend the wire up (Figure 1).

4 With your hands, loop the wire back down, making a smaller loop than the first fold (Figure 2).

5 Repeat steps 3 and 4 with the wire on the other side of the first fold (Figure 3).

6 Holding the wire together near the ends, wrap four times around the loops, with the remaining wire. Cut close to the wrap on the back side of the piece. Use the round nose pliers to curl the remaining ends in slightly (Figure 4).

7 Use the chain nose pliers to pinch the three tall loops as shown in Figure 5, creating the angled shape of the loops. Flatten the loops and tails slightly.

8 Use wire, threaded from the back of the mesh on the box, to attach the wire element to the mesh. Twist the wire on the back of the mesh, cut it about ⅛" long and fold it over, hiding it behind the wrapping on the fleur-de-lis.

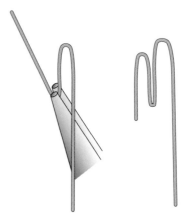

Figure 1   Figure 2

Figure 3

Figure 4

Figure 5

To make charm on needlepoint project:

1 Using the 16-gauge wire, follow the directions for mesh box project on the previous page through step 6, making the loops a little larger.

2 Flatten the loops with the chasing hammer and bench block.

3 Sew to your needlework to accent the design.

Woven Picture Frame

FINISHED SIZE:
Approximately 2¼" wide x 2¾" tall.

H ere is a fun way to add a finishing touch to a small picture for the refrigerator door. With all the wire colors available, you have many choices to bring out the colors in any photograph. Or braid it in red and green, and you could hang it from the Christmas tree.

YOU WILL NEED

- 3 feet of 26-gauge craft wire in pale green and dark blue
- Three 3-foot lengths of 26-gauge craft wire pin purple and green
- Adhesive-backed magnetic sheeting
- Glue
- Scissors
- Photograph
- Pencil
- Wire cutters
- Clamp

1 Fold all the lengths of wire in half and clamp together side by side (Figure 1).

2 Begin weaving, as shown, keeping all the wires in each set of four side by side with no overlapping, except for the braiding (Figure 2).

3 When the braid is 7¾" long, unclamp the beginning of the braid and bend the braid into an oval. Wind the tail wires around where the ends meet. Glue in place, if necessary.

4 Center the braided frame over the photograph, outlining the braid with pencil.

5 Cut the photograph ¹⁄₁₆" inside the pencil mark.

6 Use the photo as a template to trace the shape onto the magnetic sheeting.

7 Adhere the photo to the sheeting and glue the frame around the photo.

Figure 1

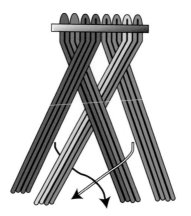

Figure 2

Spiral Penholders

These fun and funky pen and pencil holders go perfectly with a calendar of cartoons! They're so easy to make and fun to boing around while reading the daily chuckles.

FINISHED SIZE:
Approximately 3½" to 4" tall.

YOU WILL NEED

- About 1½ feet of various bright-colored 16-gauge craft wires
- Round nose pliers
- Wire cutters
- Wood base, painted and varnished (at least ½" thick and large enough for the calendar plus about 5" for the holders)
- Cartoon calendar
- Glue
- Notepad
- ⅜" x 5" wood dowel
- Drill

1 Using the round nose pliers, curl the end of one of the wires into a spiral (Figure 1).

2 Holding the spiral flat on the side of the dowel, wind the wire around the dowel for about 3½". Bend the tail of the wire in line with the dowel (Figure 2).

3 Slide the wire off the dowel and cut ⅜" from the bend.

4 Repeat for the other colored wires.

5 Drill a ⅜" deep hole in the wood base for each penholder.

6 Glue the holders in place.

7 Glue calendar to wood base.

Figure 1

Figure 2

Tip

This project and the Desk Organizer that follows (page 98) are fun, easy, and especially rewarding for children since they can have fun and make something useful at the same time. They are great projects to make as a family for gift-giving.

Desk Organizer with Miniature Toy

FINISHED SIZE:
Wire toy, approximately 3" wide x 2½" deep x 4½" tall.

I've seen one of these bead maze toys in every children's waiting room from the doctor's office to the hair cutter's salon. Simple, yet fun, their bright colors and large beads moving along the wire are always something kids love to play with. But I think they are sort of fun, too.

And this miniature one is so easy to make, I can have one in every room! This toy will be fiddled with by young and old alike—while they chat on the phone or try to think of what to write.

You can go beyond this one and make an elaborate one that rises up high like a roller coaster or long like a dragon. The possibilities are just endless.

YOU WILL NEED

- 1½ feet of 20-, 18-, or 16-gauge wire in four bright colors
- About 24 bright-colored size 6 beads (or any that will slide easily on the wire)
- Wood base, painted and varnished (at least ½" thick with about 8" x 11" surface, depending on pencil holder and notepad used)
- Pen and pencil holder
- Notepad holder
- Wire cutters
- Glue
- Drill

1 Drill eight ⅜" deep holes in the upper left corner of the wood in two rows of four, ¾" apart and ½" from the edge (Figure 1).

2 Glue one wire in each of the four holes in one row. Let the glue dry completely.

3 Thread the beads onto the wire in random order, putting about five or six beads on each wire.

4 Loop one wire around a pencil a few times, slide the pencil out, and then glue the end of the wire into one of the holes in the other row—not necessarily the one directly opposite.

5 Loop another wire around the first, leaving plenty of space between the wires for sliding the beads. Glue the second wire in one of the holes in the other row. Repeat for the last two wires.

6 Glue the pen and pencil holder, as well as the notepad holder, in place.

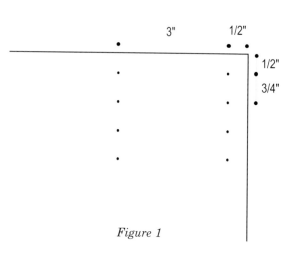

Figure 1

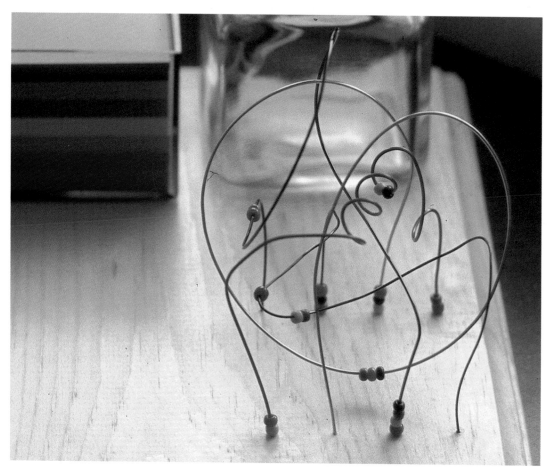

Bookmarks

FINISHED SIZE:
Varying from ½" to 1" wide and from 1½" to 3" tall.

These five designs for bookmarks are fun to construct and add a personal touch when tucked into a book wrapped up for a friend or loved one.

YOU WILL NEED

- About 16" of 20-gauge colored craft wire
- Round nose pliers
- Chain nose pliers
- Wire cutters
- Chasing hammer (optional)
- Pounding block (optional

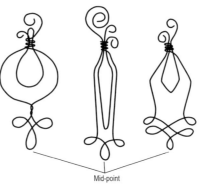

1   2   3

Patterns 1, 2, and 3

1 Beginning at the mid-point on the pattern and the middle of the wire (Figure 1), make three loops in the wire (Figure 2).

Mid-point

Figure 1

Figure 2

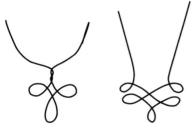

Figure 3

2 For Pattern 1, twist the wires together, and for Pattern 3, make the two more loops (Figure 3). You don't do anything here for Pattern 2.

3 Bend one end of the wires up one side of the pattern, make the center loop, and go back up to the top (Figure 4).

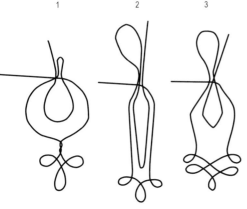

Figure 4

4 Bend the other end of the wire up and over to the other side (Figure 5).

5 Then, grasping the wires with the chain nose pliers, wind the tail around all three wires (Figure 6). Cut close to the wrap.

6 Cut the top wires at varying lengths and loosely spiral.

7 Flatten with a chasing hammer and pounding block, if desired.

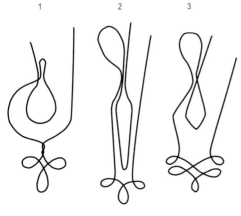

Figure 5

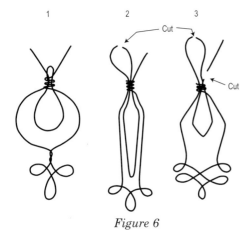

Figure 6

Patterns 4 and 5

1 Beginning at the mid-point indicated on the pattern (Figure 7), use the round nose pliers to fold the wire in half.

2 Carefully bend the wire to the pattern. For Pattern 5, cut ends 3½" from point A and spiral each end. For Pattern 4, twist the ends together for ⅜", cut the ends 1¾" long, and loosely spiral each end.

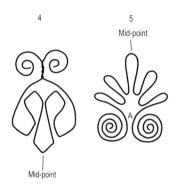

Figure 7

Cat Silhouette Votive Candleholder Accent

Here is a quick way to add a decorative element to a votive candleholder, to show your love of our feline friends or to set the mood at Halloween.

Because the accent is easily removed from the votive, this project can be adapted to other accents to make the changing seasons or holiday; you can change to stars, a turkey, or any silhouette you find from cookie cutters to children's coloring books.

YOU WILL NEED

- Black 18-gauge soft wire
- Round nose pliers
- Wire cutters
- Votive candleholder

1 Beginning about 6" from one end of the wire, bend the wire to match the cat in the pattern (Figure 1).

2 Coil the wire ends a little smaller than the candleholder, so the wire grabs the candleholder and stays in place.

3 Slide onto the votive candleholder, adjusting, if necessary, so that there is no wire leaning over the inside of the holder where it might get damaged from the candle flame.

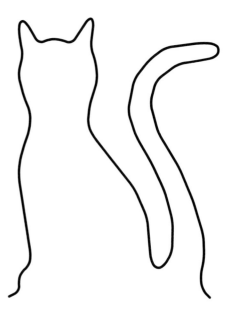

Figure 1

Christmas Ball with Stars

FINISHED SIZE:
2½" ball.

The technique used in this project is the same as the wooden boxes on pages 78-83. Here, stars float on a midnight blue sky, on this easy to complete painted papier-mâché ball. With all the papier-mâché shapes available at the craft stores, you could really take off with this idea—from balls to rocking horses to little picture frames!

YOU WILL NEED

- Papier-mâché Christmas ball, painted and varnished
- Varied sizes of scrap gold-toned wire
- Chain nose pliers
- Super Glue®
- Toothpick

1 Bend wire into a five-pointed zigzag (Figure 1).

2 Bend each point, as shown, to the shape of a star (Figure 2). Make different sizes. Pound some flat.

3 Bend the stars gently to fit the curve of the ball.

4 Hold in place with a toothpick and drip the glue onto the wire so it seeps onto the ball and glues the star in place. Repeat for each star.

Figure 1

Figure 2

Copper Star

FINISHED SIZE:
6¼".

Extend your wirework projects out into the garden with this bold copper design. You also can hang bells or chimes from the bottom three points of the star to make a wind chime to hang at your back door. Or make it smaller, in gold or silver, and hang on the tree at Christmastime.

YOU WILL NEED

- 5 feet of 14-gauge soft copper wire
- One spool of 22-gauge soft copper wire
- Round nose pliers
- Chain nose pliers
- Wire cutters

1 With the round nose pliers, make an open spiral about ½" wide.

2 Lay the spiral over (Figure 1) and make the two bends with the round nose pliers. Cut the wire, as shown, and curl the end into another spiral. Make five more.

3 Follow the pattern in Figure 2 to make the center spiral.

4 Using the 22-gauge wire, join the pieces together, one at a time, by wrapping the wires (Figure 3).

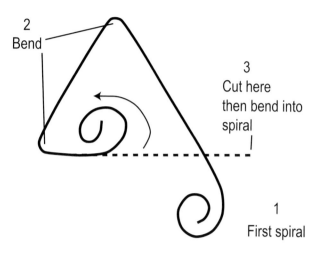

Figure 1

Figure 2

Figure 3

Wooden Star Ornaments

FINISHED SIZE:
3¾".

These wooden stars add a little weaving to the idea begun with the Christmas Ball with Stars on pages 106-107. The weaving is simple and the little decorative shapes finish off the design. The glue on the metallic paint gives you the option of an antique look or something that's bright and shiny.

YOU WILL NEED

- 3" flat wooden star shape, painted or varnished
- One spool of 26-gauge wire (gold, silver, or yellow)
- Round nose pliers
- Tacky Glue® or Super Glue® (for antique look on gold paint)

1 Working from the spool, hold the end of the wire at the back of the wooden star and begin wrapping over the base of two points of the star and behind the base of one (Figure 1). Repeat around until the weaving is about ½" wide.

2 Cut the wire so it ends at the back of the star, and glue in place with tacky glue.

3 Make spirals, stars or curlicues and glue at the center and points of the stars.

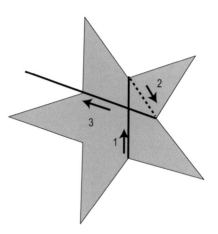

Figure 1

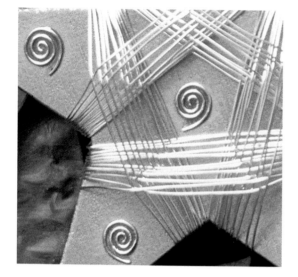

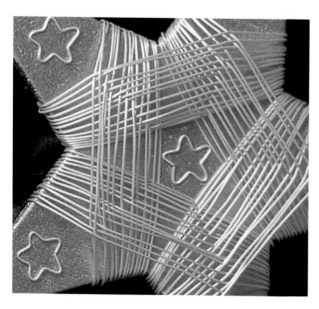

Teal and Silver Beaded Snowflake

FINISHED SIZE:
Approximately 4¼".

A dding beads to wire projects always opens up more possibilities for color and texture. This snowflake can have many different looks, depending on the color of wire and the beads you choose.

YOU WILL NEED

- One spool of 26-gauge teal green soft wire
- One spool of 24-gauge soft silver-toned wire
- 186 size 8 teal seed beads
- Round nose pliers
- Chain nose pliers
- Pin vise
- Wire cutters
- Masking tape
- Scissors
- Ruler

1 Cut six 15" lengths of green wire. Fold each one in half and twist with the pin vise and half-round pliers. Cut to 12" and fold at center to 60-degree angle (Figure 1).

2 Cut six 6" lengths of the green wire and fold at the center to 60-degree angle as shown in Figure 1.

3 Cut six 8" lengths of the silver wire and fold at the center to 60-degree angle as well.

4 Arrange the wires as shown in Figure 2. Take some time to adjust the wires so they follow the pattern. Tape a piece of masking tape over the center of the pattern to hold the wires temporarily together.

5 Using the green wire, wrap around each set of wires ½" from the center as indicated in Figure 2.

6 Bend the two single green wires together in each "V" of the design and twist them together about three times around (Figure 3).

7 Thread three beads on each wire and twist each of the two wires together again. Cut each wire to about ½" and curl into a spiral with the tip of the round nose pliers (Figure 4).

8 Now thread six beads onto the silver wires on either side of the twisted green wire.

9 Using the green wire, wrap four times tightly around the silver and twisted green wires (Figure 5). Repeat for the other sets of wire.

Continued on next page

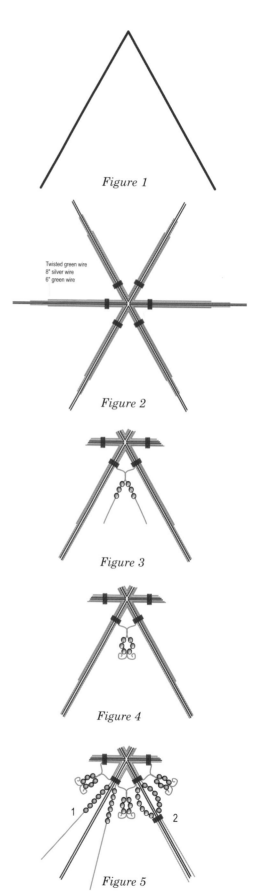

Figure 1

Twisted green wire
8" silver wire
6" green wire

Figure 2

Figure 3

Figure 4

Figure 5

Figure 6

Figure 7

Figure 8

10 Bend the two silver wires together in each "V" of the design and twist them together about three times around (Figure 6).

11 Thread six beads on each wire and twist each of the two wires together again. Cut each wire to about ½" and curl into a spiral with the tip of the round nose pliers (Figure 7).

12 Cut the green twisted wire to ¾" and curl into large, loose spirals.

13 Cut a 12" length of green wire and wrap it twice around the center of the snowflake.

14 Slide a bead onto the wire and wrap the wire around the next spoke of the snowflake (Figure 8). Repeat around so there are six beads around the center of the snowflake.

15 Wind the green wire twice around the last spoke and cut.

Brass Square Wire Snowflake

FINISHED SIZE:
Approximately 4¼".

I made this snowflake for an ornament exchange with my friends, Elizabeth Gourley and her twin sister, Ellen Talbott. I like the way the square wire reflects the light. You could enhance the reflective qualities by twisting some of the square wire before beginning the project.

YOU WILL NEED

- 8 feet of 20-gauge square soft wire
- 2 feet of 20-gauge round soft wire
- Round nose pliers
- Chain nose pliers
- Wire cutters
- Ruler

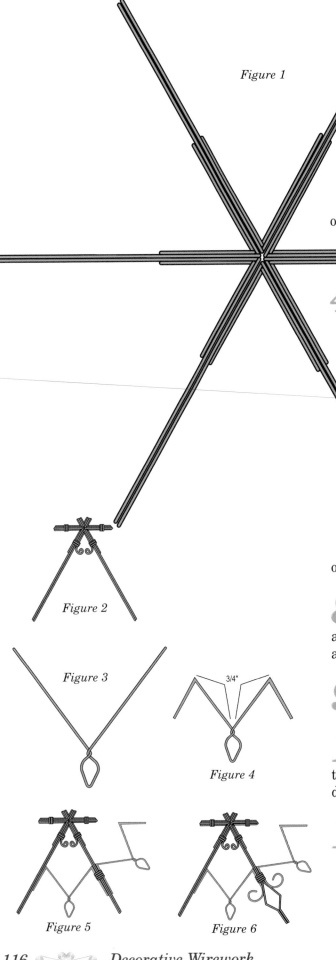

Figure 1

1 Cut six sets of wire: 6", 5", and 2½" long.

2 Fold each wire in half to 60-degree angles. Adjust the 6" and 2½" wires to fit on the pattern as shown (Figure 1).

3 Pick up two sets of wire and wrap four times with the round wire, about ½" from the center of the snowflake.

4 Pick up the next set and wrap it to one of the unwrappedsides of the first two sets. Repeat around until you join the first set to the last.

5 With the round nose pliers, curl the ends of the short lengths of wire into ¼"-wide loose spirals (Figure 2).

6 Grab one of the 5" wires in the center and bend it into an elongated loop. Twist the wires around once at the base of the loop (Figure 3).

7 Bend as shown ¾" away from the twist. Repeat for the other five 5" wires (Figure 4).

8 Hold two of the 5" wires on either side of one of the spokes of the snowflake and wrap four times around with the round wire (Figure 5). Repeat around the snowflake.

9 Trim the ends of the 5" wires to about ½" and curl intoloose spirals.

10 Bend the 6" wires away from each other, then into diamond shapes (Figure 6). Wrap three times around the top of the diamond shape.

11 Trim the ends to about ½" and curl into loose spirals.

Figure 2

Figure 3

Figure 4

3/4"

Figure 5

Figure 6

FINISHED SIZE:
Approximately 4¼".

This easy-to-make snowflake will have its own special look, determined by the beads you choose. Because it's so quick to make, you could easily make several for gift exchanges, to dress up the top of a package, or just to add to your own home decorations.

Be sure to check that all the beads slide easily onto the 20-gauge wire before beginning.

YOU WILL NEED

- 15 feet of 20-gauge soft silver-colored wire
- 24 feet of 22-gauge soft silver-colored wire
- 18 ⅝"-long bugle beads
- 18 size 6 seed beads
- 24 small Delica beads
- Six ⅜"-long oval beads
- Six 5mm-long rectangular beads
- Six ⅝"-long oval beads
- Round nose pliers
- Wire cutters

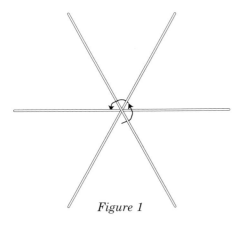

Figure 1

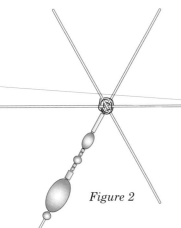

Figure 2

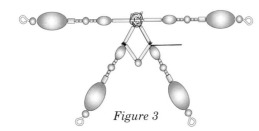

Figure 3

1 Cut the 20-gauge wire into three 5" lengths and arrange as in Figure 1.

2 Weave the 22-gauge wire over and under the center of the snowflake two to three times around, locking the wires together. Cut.

3 Following the bead pattern (Figure 2), thread the beads onto a spoke of the wire, and then loop the wire end to hold the beads in place. You may need to take some time to straighten any bends in the wire so that the bugle beads will slide easily onto the wire. Repeat for each spoke of the snowflake.

4 Wind the 22-gauge wire around one of the spokes after the first bead strung.

5 String one bugle bead, one size 6 bead, and one more bugle bead. Bend the wire as shown (Figure 3) and wind it around the next spoke of the snowflake. Repeat this process between each pair of spokes.

6 Wind the wire around the first spoke and cut close to the finished snowflake.

FINISHED SIZE:
Approximately 5½".

There's something to be said for saving the best for last; this is my favorite snowflake. The lines reaching out from the six arms of the form seem to be the classic snowflake shape I think of when I imagine the real thing. I also like the shiny silver wire.

YOU WILL NEED

- 12 feet of 18-gauge soft silver-colored wire
- 1 foot of 24-gauge soft silver-colored wire
- 5 feet of 20-gauge soft silver-colored wire

- Round nose pliers
- Wire cutters
- Ruler

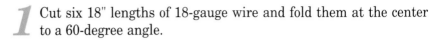

1 Cut six 18" lengths of 18-gauge wire and fold them at the center to a 60-degree angle.

2 With the 24-gauge wire, weave the lengths together at the center, by winding over and under each set of two, twice around (Figure 1).

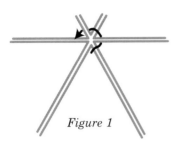

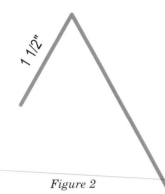

Figure 1

3 Cut six 6" lengths of 18-gauge wire and fold them, 1½" from one end of the wire, to a 60-degree angle (Figure 2).

4 Fit each wire into the "V" of the snowflake.

5 With the 20-gauge wire, wrap four times around each of the spokes of the snowflake, about ½" from the center.

6 Using the round nose pliers, make a large loose spiral with the long end of the 6" lengths of wire (Figure 3).

1 1/2"

Figure 2

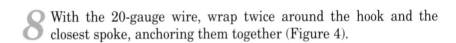

7 Bend the short length over the spiral and make a small hook.

8 With the 20-gauge wire, wrap twice around the hook and the closest spoke, anchoring them together (Figure 4).

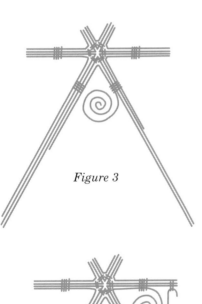

Figure 3

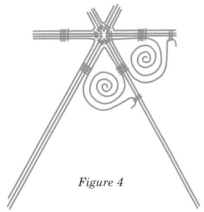

Figure 4

9 With the 20-gauge wire, wrap three times around the remaining two wires of each of the spokes 3½" from the center of the snowflake.

10 Bend the wires down over the wrap, making two small loops. Wrap three times around where they meet (Figure 5).

11 Bend each wire out again and then fold them back in about ½" away from the last wrap (Figure 6). Wrap three times around where they meet. Repeat this two more times, making a 1" fold and a ¾" fold.

12 Trim the ends to about ½" and curl into small loose spirals. Bend the folds into curves as shown in the photo.

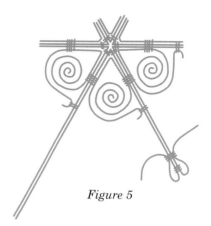

Figure 5

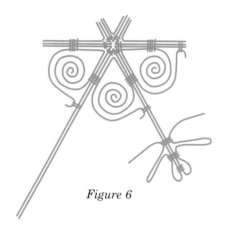

Figure 6

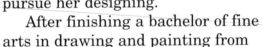

About the Author

J ane Davis has been involved in arts and crafts throughout her life. From a fourth grade poster project of the California state seal to a high school jewelry piece that was included in a Los Angeles County Museum of Art exhibit, she has been encouraged by teachers and family members to pursue her designing.

After finishing a bachelor of fine arts in drawing and painting from Long Beach State University, Jane ended up in payroll and programming, and then busy at home, raising three boys.

In 1997, she was struck by the beading bug, after seeing some beadwork bags her friend, Liz Gourley, was making. Suddenly, she had found her niche.

Carole Tripp at Creative Castle in Newbury Park, California, supported Jane's idea to self-publish a book called *Beaded Boxes*, and the same year, Jane co-wrote *Art of Seed Beading* (Sterling, 1999) with Gourley and her twin sister, Ellen Talbott.

Since then, Jane has fallen in love with writing books about arts and crafts, always looking for new mediums to express her design ideas. She has self-published two other books—*Beaded Candle Holders* and *Bead Netted Patterns*—and then wrote *The Complete Guide To Beading Techniques* (Krause, 2001) and *The Weekend Crafter: Crochet* (Lark, 2001).

Jane lives in Ventura, California, with her family and stays busy with design contributions to *Knitters* and *Vogue Knitting* magazines while teaching beadwork classes at Creative Castle and working on a knitting with beads book and another crochet book. She will be presenting some of her projects on PBS' *Creative Living* with Sheryl Borden.

Bibliography

The Wire Artist Magazine
P.O. Box 21105
Strattford, Ontario
Canada, N5A 7V4
(519) 461-1902
A magazine devoted to the design of jewelry, using
precise measuring and bending of primarily sterling
and gold-filled square wire and semiprecious stones
and gems, for high-end jewelry. It has inspiring
issues with detailed how-tos of both beginner and
advanced projects in every issue.

Clegg, Helen and Mary Larom. *Making Wire Jewelry*.
Asheville, North Carolina, Lark Books, 1997.
This is a good project book for jewelry with thick wire.

Dipasquale, Dominic. *Jewelry Making an Illustrated
Guide to Technique*. Englewood Cliffs, New Jersey,
Prentice-Hall, Inc., 1975
Sometimes the old books are the best. This has some
good information on the properties of metal, though
it deals with cast and soldered jewelry, rather than
craft wire.

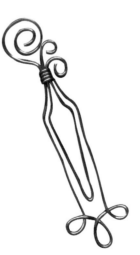

Lareau, Mark. *All Wired Up*. Loveland, Colorado,
Interweave Press, 2000.
This book has a good how-to section for basic shapes
used in most wirework.

McGuire, Barbara. *Wire in Design: Modern Wire Art and
Mixed Media*. Iola, Wisconsin, Krause Publications,
2001
This is a wonderful overview of the many types of
wirework to explore, with beautiful photos of work
from a broad range of styles to inspire.

Supply Sources

I encourage you to seek out local sources for your supplies as much as possible. Nothing compares to seeing a product before you buy it, plus it's so much fun to look at all the cool stuff at bead stores and jewelry supply stores and imagine all the things you could make. However, if you can't find supplies locally, here are some mail-order sources for supplies used for projects in this book.

Artistic Wire
752 North Larch Avenue
Elmhurst, IL 60126
(630) 530-7567
www.artisticwire.com
Makers of a huge selection of colored craft wire, as well
    as craft jigs, tools, and how-to videos. Most of the
    projects in this book were made from this wire.

Creative Castle
2321 Michael Drive
Newbury Park, CA 91320
(805) 499-1377
www.creativecastle.com
A bead store that caters to wirework as well, carrying a
    large selection of craft and silver wire and tools for
    the wirework crafter, including pin vises, jigs, and a
    great selection of pliers and wire cutters.

Fire Mountain Gems
#1 Fire Mountain Way
Grants Pass, OR 97526
(800) 423-2319
www.firemountaingems.com
Mail-order company with a wonderful catalog showing its
    large selection of jewelry-making supplies, including
    findings, silver, niobium, and gold-filled wire, and
    tools.

TSI, Inc.
101 Nickerson Street
P.O. Box 9266
Seattle, WA 98109
(800) 426-9984
www.tsijeweltools.com
Has all you need for jewelry-making, from pliers and
    cutters to power tools and kilns.

Index

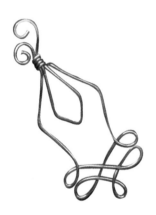

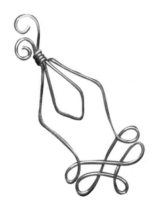

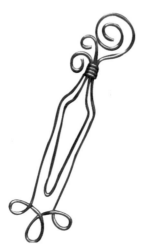